Top 10 Email Service Providers Keyboard Shortcuts

By

U. C-Abel Books.

Published by U. C-Abel Books

Table of Contents.

Chapter 5 Tips, Tricks, Techniques, and Keyboard Shortcuts for use in

Acknowledgement.

We really thank the following companies: Yahoo Corporation (represented by Yahoomail), Fastmail Pty Ltd (represented by Fastmail), Apple Inc. (represented by iCloud Mail), Microsoft Corporation (represented by Outlook Mail), GMX Internet Services (represented by GMX Mail), AOL Inc. (represented by AOL Mail), Yandex N.V. (represented by Yandex Mail), Zoho Corporation Pvt. Ltd. (represented by Zoho Mail), Hush Communications Corp. (represented by Hushmail), and Google Inc. (represented by Gmail) for making some of the keyboard shortcuts and tips we listed in this book available to us. These companies are great indeed because it's only their kind that will include and make ready keyboard shortcuts to users knowing how crucial they are.

Dedication

We dedicate this piece of work to users of email service providers contained on the cover of this book.

Introduction

After our research, we picked these ten (10) email service providers: Yahoomail, Fastmail, Icloud Mail, Outlook Mail, GMX Mail, AOL Mail, Yandex Mail, Zoho Mail, Hushmail, and Google Mail (Gmail) for being outstanding in so many ways. We are using this medium to say a big thank you, well done, and congratulations to them, and as well advise them to keep the fire burning.

How We Began.

We enjoy using shortcuts because they set us on a high plane that astonishes people around us when we work with them. As wonderful shortcuts users, the worst eyesore we witness in computer operation is to see somebody sluggishly struggling to execute a task through mouse usage when in actual sense shortcuts will help to save that person time. Most people have asked us to help them with a list of keyboard shortcuts that can make them work as smartly as we do and that drove us into research to broaden our knowledge and truly help them as they demanded, that is the reason for the existence of this book. It is a great tool for lovers of shortcuts, and those who want to join the group.

Most times the things we love don't come by easily. It is our love for keyboard shortcuts that made us to bear long sleepless nights like owls just to make sure we get the best out of it, and it is the best we got that we are sharing with you in this book. You cannot be the same at computing after reading this book. The time you entrusted to our care is an expensive possession and we promise not to mess it up.

Thank you.

What to Know Before You Begin.

General Notes.

1. Most of the keyboard shortcuts you will see in this book refer to the U.S. keyboard layout. Keys for other layouts might not correspond exactly to the keys on a U.S. keyboard. Keyboard shortcuts for laptop computers might also differ.

2. It is important to note that when using shortcuts to perform any command, you should make sure the target area is active, if not, you may get a wrong result. Example, if you want to highlight all texts you must make sure the text field is active and if an object, make sure the object area is active. The active area is always known by the location where the cursor of your computer blinks.

3. On a Mac keyboard, the Command key is denoted with the ⌘ symbol.

4. If a function key doesn't work on your Mac as you expect it to, press the Fn key in addition to the function key. If you don't want to press the Fn key every time, you can change your Apple system preferences.

5. The plus (+) sign that comes in the middle of keyboard shortcuts simply means the keys are meant to be combined or held down together not to be added as one of the shortcut keys. In a case where plus sign is needed; it will be duplicated (++).

6. Many keyboards assign special functions to function keys, by default. To use the function key for other purposes, you have to press Fn+the function key.

7. For keyboard shortcuts in which you press one key immediately followed by another key, the keys are separated by a comma (,).

8. For chapters that have more than one topic, search for "A fresh topic" to see the beginning of a topic, and "End of Topic" to see the end of a topic.

9. It is also important to note that the keyboard shortcuts listed in this book are for the top 10 email service providers listed in this book.

10. To get more information on this title visit ucabelbooks.wordpress.com and search the site using keywords related to it.

11. Our chief website is under construction.

Some Short Forms You Will Find in This Book and Their Full Meaning.

Here are short forms used in this Top 10 Email Service Provider Keyboard Shortcuts book and their full meaning.

1.	Win	-	Windows logo key
2.	Tab	-	Tabulate Key
3.	Shft	-	Shift Key
4.	Prt sc	-	Print Screen
5.	Num Lock	-	Number Lock Key
6.	F	-	Function Key
7.	Esc	-	Escape Key
8.	Ctrl	-	Control Key
9.	Caps Lock	-	Caps Lock Key
10.	Alt	-	Alternate Key

Email Service Providers included in this book.

The information included in this book is for the following ESPs:

1. Yahoomail.
2. Fastmail.
3. Icloud Mail.
4. Outlook Mail.
5. GMX Mail.
6. AOL Mail.
7. Yandex Mail.
8. Zoho Mail.
9. Hushmail.
10. Google Mail (Gmail).

CHAPTER 1.

Fundamental Knowledge of Keyboard Shortcuts.

Without the existence of the keyboard, there wouldn't have been anything like keyboard shortcuts so in this chapter we will learn a little about the computer keyboard before moving to keyboard shortcuts.

1. Definition of Computer Keyboard.

This is an input device that is used to send data to computer memory.

Sketch of a Keyboard

1.1 Types of Keyboard.

   i. Standard (Basic) Keyboard.

ii. Enhanced (Extended) Keyboard.

i. **Standard Keyboard:** This is a keyboard designed during the 1800s for mechanical typewriters with just 10 function keys (F keys) placed at the left side of it.

ii. **Enhanced Keyboard:** This is the current 101 to 102-key keyboard that is included in almost all the personal computers (PCs) of nowadays, which has 12 function keys, usually at the top side of it.

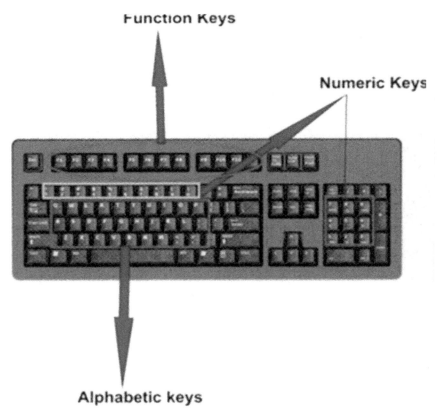

1.2 Segments of the keyboard

- Numeric keys.
- Alphabetic keys.
- Punctuation keys.
- Windows Logo key.
- Function keys.
- Special keys.

Numeric Keys: Numeric keys are keys with numbers from **0 - 9**.

Alphabetic Keys: These are keys that have alphabets on them, ranging from **A** to **Z**.

Punctuation Keys: These are keys of the keyboard used for punctuation, examples include comma, full stop, colon, question marks, hyphen, etc.

Windows Logo Key: A key on Microsoft Computer keyboard with its logo displayed on it. Search for this 🔲 on your keyboard.

Apple Key: This also known as Command key is a modifier key that you can find on an Apple keyboard. It usually has the image of an apple or command logo on it.

Search for this on your Apple keyboard 🔲

Function Keys: These are keys that have **F** on them which are usually combined with other keys. They are F1 - F12, and are also in the class called *Special Keys.*

Special Keys: These are keys that perform special functions. They include: Tab, Ctrl, Caps lock, Insert, Prt sc, alt gr, Shift, Home, Num lock, Esc, and many others. Special keys differ according to the type of computer involved. In some keyboard layout, especially laptops, the keys that turn the speaker on/off, the one that increases/decreases volume, the key that turns the computer Wifi on/off are also special keys.

Other Special Keys Worthy of Note.

Enter Key: This is located at the right-hand corner of most keyboards. It is used to send messages to the computer to execute commands, in most cases it is used to mean "Ok" or "Go".

Escape Key (ESC): This is the first key on the upper left of most keyboards. It is used to cancel routines, close menus and select options such as **Save** according to circumstances.

Control Key (CTRL): It is located on the bottom row of the left and right hand side of the keyboard. They also work with the function keys to execute commands using Keyboard shortcuts (key combinations).

Alternate Key (ALT): It is located on the bottom row also of some keyboard, very close to the CTRL key on both side of the keyboard. It enables many editing functions to be accomplished by using some keystroke combinations on the keyboard.

Shift Key: This adds to the roles of function keys. In addition, it enables the use of alternative function of a particular button (key), especially, those with more than one function on a key. E.g. use of capital letters, symbols, and numbers.

1.3. Selecting/Highlighting With Keyboard.

This is a highlighting method or style where data is selected using the computer keyboard instead of a computer mouse.

To do this:

- Move your cursor to the text or object you want to highlight, make sure that area is active,
- Hold down the shift key with one finger,
- Then use another finger to move the arrow key that points to the direction you want to highlight.

1.4 The Operating Modes Of The Keyboard.

Just like the computer mouse, keyboard has two operating modes. The two modes are Text Entering Mode and Command Mode.

a. **Text Entering Mode:** this mode gives the operator/user the opportunity to type text.
b. **Command Mode:** this is used to command the operating system/software/application to execute commands in certain ways.

2. Ways To Improve In Your Typing Skill.

1. Put Your Eyes Off The Keyboard.

This is the aspect of keyboard usage that many don't find funny because they always ask. "How can I put my eyes off the keyboard when I am running away from the occurrence of errors on my file?" My aim is to be fast, is this not going to slow me down?

Of course, there will be errors and at the same time your speed will slow down but the motive behind the introduction to this method is to make you faster than you are. Looking at your keyboard while you type can make you get a sore neck, it is better you learn to touch type because the more you type with your eyes fixed on the screen instead of the keyboard, the faster you become.

An alternative to keeping your eyes off your keyboard is to use the *"Das Keyboard Ultimate"*.

2. Errors Challenge You

It is better to fail than to not try at all. Not trying at all is an attribute of the weak and lazybones. When you make mistakes, try again because errors·are opportunities for improvement.

3. Good Posture (Position Yourself Well).
Do not adopt an awkward position while typing. You should get everything on your desk organized or arranged before sitting to type. Your posture while typing contributes to your speed and productivity.

4. Practice
Here is the conclusion of everything said above. You have to practice your shortcuts constantly. The practice alone is a way of improvement. "Practice brings improvement". Practice always.

2.1 Software That Will Help You Improve Your Typing Skill.

There are several Software programs for typing that both kids and adults can use for their typing skill. Here is a list of software that can help you improve in your typing: Mavis Beacon, Typing Instructor, Mucky Typing Adventure, Rapid Tying Tutor, Letter Chase Tying Tutor, Alice Touch Typing Tutor and many more. Personally, I love Mavis Beacon.

To learn typing using MAVIS BEACON, install Mavis Beacon software to your computer, start with keyboard lesson, then move to games. Games like *Penguin Crossing, Creature Lab*, or *Space Junk* will help you become a professional in typing. Typing and keyboard shortcuts work hand-in-hand.

Sketch of a computer mouse

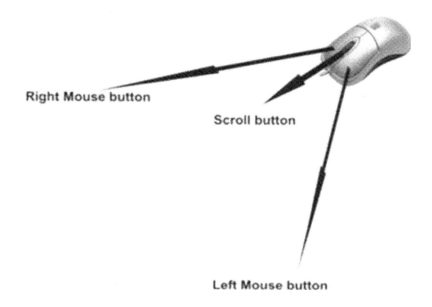

Right Mouse button

Scroll button

Left Mouse button

3. Mouse:

This is an oval-shaped portable input device with three buttons for scrolling, left clicking, and right clicking that enables work to be done effectively on a computer. The plural form of mouse is mice.

3.1 Types of Computer Mouse

- Mechanical Mouse.
- Optical Mechanical Mouse (Optomechanical).
- Laser Mouse.
- Optical Mouse.
- BlueTrack Mouse.

3.2 Forms of Clicking:

Left Clicking: This is the process of clicking the left side button of the mouse. It can also be called *clicking* without the addition of *left*.

Right Clicking: It is the process of clicking the right side button of a computer mouse.

Double Clicking: It is the process of clicking the left side button two times (twice) and immediately.

Triple Clicking: It is the process of clicking the left side button three times (thrice) and immediately.

Double clicking is used to select a word while triple clicking is used to select a sentence or paragraph.

Scroll Button: It is the little key attached to the mouse that looks like a tiny wheel. It takes you up and down a page when moved.

3.3 Mouse Pad: This is a small soft mat that is placed under the mouse to make it have a free movement.

3.4 Laptop Mouse Touchpad

This unlike the mouse we explained above is not external, rather it is inbuilt (comes with the laptop computer). With the presence of a laptop mouse touchpad, an external mouse is not needed to use a laptop, except in a case where it is malfunctioning or the operator prefers to use external one for some reasons.

The laptop mouse touchpad is usually positioned at the end of the keyboard section of a laptop computer. It is rectangular in shape with two buttons positioned below it. The two buttons/keys are used for left and right clicking just like the external mouse. Some laptops come with four mouse keys. Two placed above the mouse for left and right clicking and two other keys placed below it for the same function.

4. Definition Of Keyboard Shortcuts.

Keyboard shortcuts are defined as a series of keys, most times with combination that execute tasks which typically involve the use of mouse or other input devices.

5. Why You Should Use Shortcuts.

1.   One may not be able to use a computer mouse easily because of disability or pain.

2.   One may not be able to see the mouse pointer as a result of vision impairment, in such case what will the person do? The answer is SHORTCUT.

3.   Research has made it known that Extensive mouse usage is related to Repetitive Syndrome Injury (RSI) greatly than the use of keyboard.

4.   Keyboard shortcuts speed up computer users, making learning them a worthwhile effort.

5.   When performing a job that requires precision, it is wise that you use the keyboard instead of mouse, for

instance, if you are dealing with Text Editing, it is better you handle it using keyboard shortcuts than spending more time doing it with your computer mouse alone.

6. Studies calculate that using keyboard shortcuts allows working 10 times faster than working with the mouse. The time you spend looking for the mouse and then getting the cursor to the position you want is lost! Reducing your work duration by 10 times gives you greater results.

5.1 Ways To Become A Lover Of Shortcuts.

1. Always have the urge to learn new shortcut keys associated with the programs you use.
2. Be happy whenever you learn a new shortcut.
3. Try as much as you can to apply the new shortcuts you learnt.
4. Always bear it in mind that learning new shortcuts is worth it.
5. Always remember that the use of keyboard shortcuts keeps people healthy while performing computer activities.

5.2 How To Learn New Shortcut Keys
1. Do a research on them: quick references (a cheat sheet comprehensively compiled like ours) can go a long way to help you improve.
2. Buy applications that show you keyboard shortcuts every time you execute an action with mouse.

3. Disconnect your mouse if you must learn this fast.
4. Read user manuals and help topics (Whether offline or online).

5.3 Your Reward For Knowing Shortcut Keys.
1. You will get faster unimaginably.
2. Your level of efficiency will increase.
3. You will find it easy to use.
4. Opportunities are high that you will become an expert in what you do.
5. You won't have to go for **Office button**, click **New,** click **Blank and Recent**, and click **Create** just to insert a fresh/blank page. **Ctrl +N** takes care of that in a second.

A Funny Note: Keyboarding and Mousing are in a marital union with Keyboarding being the head, so it will be unfair for anybody to put asunder between them.

5.4 Why We Emphasize On The Use of Shortcuts.
You may never leave your mouse completely unless you are ready to make your brain a box of keyboard shortcuts which will really be frustrating, just imagine yourself learning all shortcuts that go with the programs you use and their various versions. You shouldn't learn keyboard shortcuts that way.

Why we are emphasizing on the use of shortcuts is because mouse usage is becoming unusually common and unhealthy, too. So we just want to make sure both are combined so you can get fast, productive and healthy in your computer activities. All you need to know is just the most important ones associated with the programs you use.

CHAPTER 2.

15 (Fifteen) Special Keyboard Shortcuts.

The fifteen special keyboard shortcuts are fifteen (15) shortcuts every computer user should know.

The following is a list of keyboard shortcuts every computer user should know:

1. **Ctrl + A:** Control A, highlights or selects everything you have in the environment where you are working.
    If you are like **"Wow, the content of this document is large and there is no time to select all of it, besides, it's going to mount pressure on my computer?"** *Using the mouse for this is an outdated method of handling a task like selecting all, Ctrl+A will take care of that in a second.*

2. **Ctrl + C:** Control C copies any highlighted or selected element within the work environment.
    Saves the time and stress which would have been used to right click and click again just to copy. Use ctrl+c.

3. **Ctrl + N:** Control N opens a new window or file.
   Instead of clicking **File, New, blank/ template** *and another* **click,** *just press* ***Ctrl + N*** *and a fresh page or window will appear instantly.*

4. **Ctrl + O:** Control O opens a new program.
   Use ctrl +O when you want to locate / open a file or program.

5. **Ctrl + P:** Control P prints the active document.
   Always use this to locate the printer dialog box, and thereafter print.

6. **Ctrl + S:** Control S saves a new document or file and changes made by the user.
   Please stop! Don't use the mouse. Just press Ctrl+S and everything will be saved.

7. **Ctrl +V:** Control V pastes copied elements into the active area of the program in use.
   Using ctrl+V in a case like this Saves the time and stress of right clicking and clicking again just to paste.

8. **Ctrl + W:** Control W is used to close the page you are working on when you want to leave the work environment.

"There is a way Debby does this without using the mouse. Oh my God, why didn't I learn it then?" Don't worry, I have the answer. Debby presses Ctrl+W to close active windows.

9. **Ctrl + X:** Control X cuts elements (making the elements to disappear from their original place). The difference between cutting and deleting elements is that in Cutting, what was cut doesn't get lost permanently but prepares itself so that it can be pasted on another location defined by the user.

    *Use ctrl+x when you think **"this shouldn't be here and I can't stand the stress of retyping or redesigning it on the rightful place it belongs"**.*

10. **Ctrl + Y:** Control Y undoes already done actions.

    Ctrl+Z brought back what you didn't need? Press Ctrl+ Y to remove it again.

11. **Ctrl + Z:** Control Z redoes actions.
    Can't find what you typed now or a picture you inserted, it suddenly disappeared or you mistakenly removed it? Press Ctrl+Z to bring it back.

12. **Alt + F4:** Alternative F4 closes active windows or items.

    *You don't need to move the mouse in order to close an active window, just press **Alt + F4**.*

Also use it when you are done or you don't want somebody who is coming to see what you are doing.

13. **Ctrl + F6:** Control F6 Navigates between open windows, making it possible for a user to see what is happening in windows that are active.

    Are you working in Microsoft Word and want to find out if the other active window where your browser is loading a page is still progressing? Use Ctrl + F6.

14. **F1:** This displays the help window.

    *Is your computer malfunctioning? Use **F1** to find help when you don't know what next to do.*

15. **F12:** This enables user to make changes to an already saved document.

    F12 is the shortcut to use when you want to change the format in which you saved your existing document, password it, change its name, change the file location or destination, or make other changes to it. It will save you time.

Note: The Control (Ctrl) key on Windows and Linux operating system is the same thing as Command (Cmmd) key on a Macintosh computer. So if you replace Control with Command key on a Mac computer for the special shortcuts listed above, you will get the same result.

CHAPTER 3.

About Email Service Providers, Terms and Tips Associated with them.

Electronic mail commonly known as email is a method of exchanging digital messages between computer users who are connected to the internet.

Emailing is a flexible, fast, effective, and reliable way to communicate with a person or group.

A fresh topic

25 Tips for Perfecting Your E-mail Etiquette.

By Lindsay Silberman on Inc.com.

Do you have bad netiquette? In other words, are you appalling colleagues with your awful e-mail manners? Clean-up your act with these etiquette tips from the experts.

In the age of the Internet, you might find yourself clicking "reply," typing up a quick response, and hitting "send" without giving so much as a thought about what you've just written. But experts agree that your e-mail behavior has the potential to sabotage your reputation both personally and professionally.

1.   Only Discuss Public Matters. We've all heard the stories about a "private" e-mail that ended up being passed around to the entire company, and in some cases, all over the Internet. One of the most important things to consider when it comes to e-mail etiquette is whether the matter you're discussing is a public one, or something that should be talked about behind closed doors. Ask yourself if the topic being discussed is something you'd write on company letterhead or post on a bulletin board for all to see before clicking "send." --**Judith Kallos**, author of *E-Mail Etiquette Made Easy, E-Mail: The Manual, and E-Mail: A Write It Well Guide*

2.   Briefly Introduce Yourself. Do not assume the person receiving your e-mail knows who you are, or remembers meeting you. If you are uncertain whether the recipient recognizes your e-mail address or name, include a simple reminder of who you are in relation to the person you are reaching out to; a formal and extensive biography of yourself is not necessary. --**Peggy Duncan**, personal productivity expert and author of *Conquer*

Email Overload with Better Habits, Etiquette, and Outlook 2007.

3. Don't "e-mail Angry." E-mailing with bad news, firing a client or vendor, expressing anger, reprimanding someone, disparaging other people in e-mails (particularly if you're saying something less than kind about your boss) are all major no-no's. Because e-mail can seem so informal, many people fall into this trap. Always remember that e-mail correspondence lasts forever. --**Lindsey Pollak**, career and workplace expert, e-mail etiquette consultant, and author of *Getting From College to Career*

4. Use Exclamation Points Sparingly. The maximum number of exclamation points in a business e-mail? One. Otherwise, you risk looking childish and unprofessional. --**Pollak**

5. Be Careful with Confidential Information. Refrain from discussing confidential information in e-mails such as someone's tax information or the particulars of a highly-sensitive business deal. Should the e-mail get into the wrong person's hands, you could face serious - even legal - repercussions. --**Peter Post**, director of the Burlington, Vermont-based Emily Post Institute, which offers etiquette advice and answers to manners questions such as wedding etiquette, parenting issues and table manners.

6. Respond in a Timely Fashion. Unless you work in some type of emergency capacity, it's not necessary to be available the instant an e-mail arrives. Depending on the nature of the e-mail and the sender, responding within 24 to 48 hours is acceptable. --**Duncan**

7.   Refrain from Sending One-liners. "Thanks," and "Oh, OK" do not advance the conversation in any way. Feel free to put "No Reply Necessary" at the top of the e-mail when you don't anticipate a response. --**Duncan**

8.   Avoid using Shortcuts to Real Words, Emoticons, Jargon, or Slang. Words from grown, business people using shortcuts such as "4 u" (instead of "for you"), "Gr8" (for great) in business-related e-mail is not acceptable. If you wouldn't put a smiley face or emoticon on your business correspondence, you shouldn't put it in an e-mail message. Any of the above has the potential to make you look less than professional. --**Duncan**

9.   Keep it Clean. Nothing annoys recipients more than when people reply and leave the messages messy, for example, an e-mail chain that includes excessive carets (>>>), or pages and pages of e-mail addresses that weren't protected using Bcc. You can get rid of carets by selecting the text, Ctrl+F to use the Find and Replace command to find a caret and replace all of them with nothing. You can get rid of all the e-mail addresses just by deleting. Clean it up, then send it. --**Duncan**

10.   Be clear in your Subject Line. With inboxes being clogged by hundreds of e-mails a day, it's crucial that your subject line gets to the point. It should be reasonably simple and descriptive of what you have written about. Expect that any e-mail with a cute, vague, or obscure subject will get trashed. Also, proof your subject line as carefully as you would proof the rest of the e-mail. --**Post**

11. Don't Get Mistaken for Spam. Avoid subject lines that are in all caps, all lower case, and those that include URLs and exclamation points - which tend to look like Spam to the recipient. --**Judith Kallos**, author of *E-Mail Etiquette Made Easy, E-Mail: The Manual, and E-Mail: A Write It Well Guide*

12. Your Subject Line must Match the Message. Never open an old e-mail, hit Reply, and send a message that has nothing to do with the previous one. Do not hesitate to change the subject as soon as the thread or content of the e-mail chain changes. --**Peggy Duncan**, personal productivity expert and author of *Conquer Email Overload with Better Habits, Etiquette, and Outlook 2007*

13. Provide a Warning When Sending Large Attachments. Sending unannounced large attachments can clog the receiver's inbox and cause other important e-mails to bounce. If you are sending something that is over 500KB, senders should ask, 'Would you mind if I sent you an attachment? When would be the best time for you?' --**Kallos**

14. No More than two Attachments, and Provide a Logical Name. Unless it's been specifically requested, refrain from sending a message with more than two attachments. Also, give the attached file(s) a logical name so the recipient knows at a glance the subject and the sender. --**Duncan**

15. Send or Copy Others Only on a Need to Know Basis. Before you click Reply All or put names on the Cc or Bcc lines, ask yourself if all the recipients need the information in your message. If they don't, why send it? Take time to send your messages to the right people. --

Duncan

16.   Beware of the "reply all." Do not hit "reply all" unless every member on the e-mail chain needs to know. You want to make sure that you are not sending everyone on a list your answer-;whether they needed to know or not. --**Duncan**

17.   Pick up the Phone. When a topic has lots of parameters that need to be explained or negotiated and will generate too many questions and confusion, don't handle it via e-mail. Also, e-mail should not be used for last minute cancellations of meetings, lunches, interviews, and never for devastating news. If you have an employee or a friend you need to deliver bad news to, a phone call is preferable. If it's news you have to deliver to a large group, e-mail is more practical. --**Duncan**

18.   Evaluate the Importance of your e-Mail. Don't overuse the high priority option. If you overuse this feature, few people will take it seriously. A better solution is to use descriptive subject lines that explain exactly what a message is about. --**Duncan**

19.   Maintain Privacy. If you're sending a message to a group of people and you need to protect the privacy of your list, you should always use "Bcc." Additionally, avoid giving out e-mail addresses to a third party (such as an Evite, newsletter, etc). Make sure that addresses you willingly hand over to third parties stay with them, especially when the service they're offering is free. --**Duncan**

20.   Keep it Short and Get to the Point. The long e-mail is a thing of the past. Write concisely, with lots of white space, so as to not overwhelm the recipient. Make sure when you look at what you're sending it doesn't look like a burden to read - feel free to use bullet points. The person reading your e-mail should not have to dig through several paragraphs in order to figure out what you're asking. You should state the purpose of the e-mail within the first two sentences. Be clear, and be up front. --**Lindsey Pollak**, career and workplace expert, e-mail etiquette consultant, and author of *Getting From College to Career*

21.   Know your Audience. Your e-mail greeting and sign-off should be consistent with the level of respect and formality of the person you're communicating with. Also, write for the person who will be reading it - if they tend to be very polite and formal, write in that language. The same goes for a receiver who tends to be more informal and relaxed. --**Lindsey Pollak**, career and workplace expert, e-mail etiquette consultant, and author of *Getting From College to Career*

22.   Always Include a Signature. You never want someone to have to look up how to get in touch with you. If you're social media savvy, include all of your social media information in your signature as well. Your e-mail signature is a great way to let people know more about you, especially when your e-mail address is does not include your full name or company. --**Pollak**

23.   Only use an Auto-responder When Necessary. An automatic response that says, "Thank you for your e-mail message. I will respond to you as soon as I can" is useless. However, one thing these messages do great is alert spammers that your e-mail is real and that they can add you to their spam list. --**Peggy Duncan**, personal productivity expert and author of *Conquer Email Overload with Better Habits, Etiquette, and Outlook 2007*

24. Train your Staff. Business owners should make sure their staff is trained in e-mail communications - don't assume they know what they're doing, and what is considered professional. Set up e-mail standards that everyone at the company should abide by. --**Pollak**

25. Your E-mail is a Reflection of you. Every e-mail you send adds to, or detracts from your reputation. If your e-mail is scattered, disorganized, and filled with mistakes, the recipient will be inclined to think of you as a scattered, careless, and disorganized businessperson. Other people's opinions matter and in the professional world, their perception of you will be critical to your success. --**Peter Post**, director of the Burlington, Vermont-based Emily Post Institute, which offers etiquette advice and answers to manners questions such as wedding etiquette, parenting issues and table manners.

End of Topic.

A fresh topic

15 Email Marketing Tips for Small Businesses by Forbes.

Kate Kiefer Lee – Contributor.

Email marketing is a great way to reach your customers where they are without spending a lot of money. But it's a big responsibility, two—people don't give their email addresses to just anyone. Thinking about starting a company newsletter? Here are some tips to keep in mind.

1. Make it easy to subscribe. Post a signup form on your homepage, blog, Facebook page, and wherever else your customers and fans are already active. You might want to collect names and birthdays (for a special offer or gift) or invite readers to join groups, but don't go crazy with the required fields. A too-long subscribe form might scare people off.

2. Tell subscribers what to expect. Whether you plan to send company updates, letters from the president, e-commerce sales, daily deals, or weekly tips, it's important to tell your readers what to expect and how often to expect it. Give them as much information as possible on your signup form, so they can decide whether they want to be on the list or not.

3. Send a welcome email. It's always smart to remind people why they're on your list and reassure them that good things are in store. You might even send new subscribers a special offer or exclusive content, as your way of thanking them for their loyalty.

4. Design your newsletter to fit your brand. Your email campaigns should match your brand's look and feel. If you're using a template, you might want to customize it to include your company's colors and logo in the header. If your emails are consistent with the rest of your company's content, then readers will feel more familiar from the start.

5. Make it Scannable. Your subscribers are busy people who get a lot of email, so it's safe to assume you *don't* have their undivided attention. Instead of one long block, break up your content into short paragraphs. Include subheadings and images to guide readers through your email and make it easier to scan, and add a teaser to the top of your newsletter to tell subscribers what's in store. If you're sending a long article, consider inserting a "read more" link so people can get to the rest when it's convenient for them. Your subject line should be to-the-point and easy to digest, too. You might even want to a/b test subject lines to see which ones perform best.

6. Send people content they want. Email newsletter services offer features like groups and segmentation to help you make your content relevant to the people reading it. If you're sending different emails for different groups (for example, a nonprofit might send separate emails to volunteers, donors, and the board of directors), then you can ask people to check a box to join a particular group on your signup form. Segmentation allows you to target certain subscribers on your list without assigning them to group. If your store is having a sale, then you could send a campaign only to people near a particular zip code, because subscribers who live in other parts of the world don't need to know about it. You can also segment by activity, email clients, e-commerce data, and more. Sending relevant content will keep your readers engaged, and engaged readers look forward to your newsletter and share it with friends.

7. Keep a publishing calendar. A regular newsletter is a commitment. If you go several months without sending anything, then your subscribers will forget about you, and they'll be more likely to delete the next email, or worse, mark it as spam. Make time to plan, write, design, and send your newsletters regularly.

8. Edit. Even editors need editors. When you're working on your publishing calendar, leave plenty of time for the editing and revision process. Once you send a campaign, it goes straight to the inbox, and you can't go back and update it. Newsletters contain meaningful content, and sloppy ones reflect poorly on the companies who send them. Grammar and style are just as important for email as they are for websites and blogs.

9. Test. Different email clients and mobile devices display emails differently. Send test emails to colleagues, or use a testing program to make sure your emails are going to look good on screens big and small. Testing reveals design mistakes before it's too late, and testing programs can predict whether or not a campaign will get caught in a spam filter. You could even set up accounts with a few different email services for easy testing. Avoid sending one big image as a campaign, and cover your bases with a plain-text option for every email.

10. Think about mobile. If a campaign doesn't show up on mobile devices, it's not going to perform very well. Everything you send should be mobile-friendly. Check out ReturnPath's <u>"Email in Motion" infographic</u> for some data that might affect the way you design your emails. One of the highlights: According to the study, 63 percent of Americans and 41 percent of Europeans would either close or delete an email that's not optimized for mobile. Might be time to start using a responsive template.

11. Know your spam rules. A lot of innocent people send spam because they didn't know any better. Put simply, you're allowed to send bulk email only to people who specifically asked to be on your mailing list. If you collected email addresses for a lunch giveaway or an event invitation, then you don't have permission to send marketing emails unless you made that clear at signup. Include an obvious unsubscribe link in every email, and don't forget to remind subscribers how they got on your list in the first place.

12. Make it shareable. Send content that people want to share, and make it easy for them to do it. Sure, subscribers can forward your campaign to friends, but that's a lot to ask. Include a public link to the web version of your campaign so people can read it outside of their email programs, and consider adding Twitter and Facebook links to your newsletter, so readers can share your content where they're already active. When *their* friends start sharing and subscribing, you'll know it's working.

13. Keep an eye on your stats. Most email newsletter services offer free reports that contain helpful information. Learn how to read and understand your reports, so you can use the stats to improve your campaigns going forward. Pay attention to your open and click rates, and identify any patterns that make those numbers go up or down. If a campaign receives a high number of unsubscribes, then try something different the next time.

14. Be friendly. Feel free to use a casual tone in your email newsletters. Since most emails come directly from one person, people expect human voices in their inboxes. There's a good chance your subscribers are already in a informal frame of mind when they're checking their email, so an overly formal or stodgy voice might seem out of place. Plus, they've given you their email address, so you're already on a first-name basis. If you collect first names on your signup form, you can dynamically include them in your email greetings.

15. Only send email if you have something to say. This one seems obvious, but too many companies start email newsletters with no plan and nothing to say. Email is simply a way to publish content—the content itself has to come first. Before starting a newsletter, make sure it's a sustainable commitment that will help you achieve your business goals. Otherwise, you'll be wasting your subscribers' time and your own time. Ask yourself: What's the goal for this kind of communication? What do we have to say? How will we measure success? Send thoughtful newsletters, and keep the focus on your company's message.

CHAPTER 4.

Tips, Tricks, Techniques, and Keyboard Shortcuts for use in Yahoo Mail.

Introduction: Yahoo Mail is a web-based email service provider launched in 1997 by the American company called Yahoo and managed by them. Yahoo email service is free for personal use, and paid for business email plans.

A fresh topic

Features of Yahoomail.

1. The Inbox.

Lets you personalize your inbox with vibrant themes and organize your mail the way that makes sense to you. Quickly access the tools you use everyday like your Calendar, Notepad, Contacts, Instant Messages, and Search. Yahoo's message toolbar and quick actions makes it simple to sort, mark, and delete emails in a few clicks. Navigation, Folders Multitasking, or Personalization.

Your Inbox, Contacts, Calendar, Notepad and Messenger are grouped together in the top left corner making it only a click away to switch between tasks. If you get a new instant message while reading an email, just click the messenger icon to open a floating window that won't make you lose your work.

2. Search

Filter through hundreds of emails in seconds. Yahoo Mail's search tool makes it simple to find the exact message, document or photo you're looking for, no matter how far back it was sent or received.

Search by name, Search by keyword, or Search the Web.

Yahoo Mail search makes it simple to find files from a specific person. When you type a name into the search box, you will see a list of suggested people ranked based on who you email with the most. Once you select the person, Yahoo's new, improved search results page can help you sort and narrow down emails, documents, and files sent from your contact to find you exactly what you need.

3. Compose

Composing an email should be both personal and productive. With Yahoo Mail, their Compose lets you create and enhance your message with beautiful link previews and formatting options. Plus with Dropbox and Flickr integration you can attach files, documents and photos quicker than ever.

Suggested Contacts, Attachments, Link Previews or Attachment Preview

Your inbox isn't just convenient, it's a great way to stay connected to the people who matter most. Yahoo Mail makes it easy to locate and email the right person when composing a message. As you type a name on the To, Cc, or Bcc line, Yahoo Mail will recommend a list of the most

relevant people and contacts for you to choose from. After you select the first person, Yahoo Mail will suggest other people you tend to email with that person, making it faster to email groups together.

4. Calendar

Yahoo Calendar has the tools you need to help manage and organize your busy schedule.

Available in calendar are: Calendar Entry, or Multiple Calendars.

Get reminders for birthdays, anniversaries, appointments, and never forget an important event again. With Yahoo Calendar, you can create calendar entries by clicking on the time and date when the event will be occurring. Add the event title, location and select Add More Details to see options to invite people to the event or to add an alert reminder.

5. Your Contacts

Keep in touch with your personal network. Yahoo's two-step import feature allows you to add contacts from your

Facebook account or other email providers like Gmail or Outlook, making it simple to switch email accounts.
Enhanced Contacts and Import Contacts

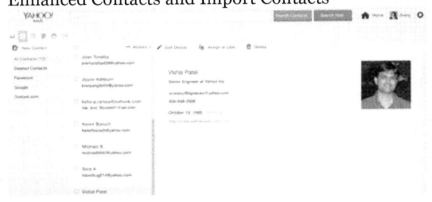

On each contact's profile, you'll find a snapshot of your most recent interactions with them including messages, photos, and files. So if you've had a long email thread with a friend about an upcoming vacation, simply navigate over to your contacts and select your friend's name to quickly see the latest emails and attachments they've sent you about the trip.

6. Storage
Yahoo Mail gives you the most free storage of any email provider. With 1TB of free space (that's 1000 GB!), you'll never have to worry about deleting emails to save space.

1 TB Storage

Keep all the emails and files sent to you. To check how much storage you have, go to Settings, and under Accounts you'll see the percent of storage you've used.

7. Security

Yahoo Mail uses the leading security technology to help keep you safe online. SSL encryption keeps your mail secure as it travels between your computer's web browser and Yahoo's servers. This means no matter where you are, whether you're at home or browsing your mail in a coffee shop, your mail information is kept safe.

SSL

Anytime you use Yahoo Mail - whether it's on the web, mobile web, mobile apps, or via IMAP, POP or SMTP - it is 100% encrypted by default and protected with 2,048 bit certificates. This encryption extends to your emails, attachments, contacts, as well as Calendar and Messenger in Mail.

8. Spam Filters.

Yahoo Mail blocks over 15 billion spam messages daily. Yahoo uses machine learning and constantly tunes and improves their filtering technologies that block spam and other malicious emails you do not want to see. You can help train the filters by clicking on the Spam button every time you encounter unwanted emails in your inbox.

End of Topic.

A fresh topic

The Starting Point of Shortcuts in Yahoo Mail.

Yahoo Mail is designed to support assistive technologies, like screen readers. While using these accessibility features, you can use keyboard shortcuts to navigate your Yahoo Mail messages.

Use keyboard shortcuts in Yahoo Mail.

Go to your Inbox

While in Yahoo Mail:

- Press the **m** key on your keyboard to go to your Inbox.
  - If the virtual cursor is on, you'll need to bypass it first.
- Once the Inbox is loaded, the first email in it has focus and the virtual cursor will be off.

Move through your Inbox

- Press the **Tab key** twice to move focus to the mailbox.
- Use the **up/down arrow keys** to move through the rows in the table.
  - When you press the **down** key, the next row is focused.

- ○ When you press the **up** key, the previous row is focused.
- ○ The screen reader should read the contents of each row from left-to-right.

Opening an email

Once an email is selected:

- Press the **Enter** key.
  - ○ The email opens and the email header has focus.m
  - ○ The virtual cursor should automatically toggle on.
- Use the **up/down arrow keys** to scroll through the message.
- Use the **right/left arrow keys** to go to the next or previous message.
  -
  - ○ When you press the **right** key, you go to the next message.
  - ○ When you press the **left** key, you go to the previous message.

End of Topic.

39

A fresh topic ⌐↳

Keyboard Shortcuts in Yahoo Mail.

Yahoo Mail offers a variety of keyboard shortcuts to navigate, send, view email, and much more. We've got them all right here.

These keyboard shortcuts are for Windows operating systems. Most shortcuts will also work on Macs by substituting **Cmd** (Mac) for **Ctrl** (Windows).

Use the following list of keyboard shortcuts to enhance your productivity in Yahoo mail.

Keyboard Shortcuts with Conversations Enabled.

Working with Conversations.

Shortcut	Action
Up/Down	Highlight the next conversation up or down
Comma	Highlight the next conversation up
Period	Highlight the next conversation down
Enter or Return	Open a conversation
Spacebar	Check/Uncheck a conversation
Shift+R	Reply to a conversation

Shift+A	Reply all to a conversation
Shift+F	Forward a conversation
K	Mark as read/unread
L	Star/Unstar a conversation
Ctrl+A	Select all conversations in view
Ctrl+Up/Down	Move focus up or down the list (preserving selection)
D	Open Move menu
D then 1-9	Move conversation(s) to one of your first 9 folders
Ctrl+Shift+E	Create a new folder
D then Ctrl+Shift+E	Move conversation(s) to a new folder
Shift+C	Add sender to contacts
[left arrow]	Previous conversation
[right arrow]	Next conversation
[	Move to the previous tab
]	Move to the next tab

Working with individual cards in a Conversation.

Shortcut	Action
Comma	Highlight the previous card within a conversation
Period	Highlight the next card within a conversation
Enter, Spacebar	Expand/collapse a card
R	Reply to a card
A	Reply all to a card
F	Forward a card

| Shift+K | Mark a card as read/unread |
| Shift+L | Star/Unstar a card |

General Commands.

Shortcut	Action
Delete	Sends the selected messages to the Trash.
E	Archives the selected messages.
M	Check mail (jumps to Inbox)
Shift+M	Check all mail (includes POP accounts)
N	Start a new email conversation
I	Start a new Instant Message (IM)
T	Start a new SMS message (text)
V	Toggle Preview Pane
S	Search

Compose.

Shortcut	Action
Ctrl+Shift+U	Attach files (one at a time)
Ctrl+S	Save as a draft
Ctrl+Enter	Send message
Ctrl+U	Underline
Ctrl+B	Bold
Ctrl+I	Italics
Alt+Shift+5	Strikethrough
Ctrl+Shift+E	Center text
Ctrl+Shift+L	Align Left

Ctrl+Shift+R	Align Right

Attachment Previews.

Shortcut	Action
[left arrow]	Previous attachment
[right arrow]	Next attachment
Up/Down	Scroll through an attachment
Ctrl+F	Switches to expanded view from side by side mode
Esc	Returns to previous mode
Ctrl+[++]	Zooms in on a document
Ctrl+[--]	Zooms out on a document

Keyboard Shortcuts with Conversations Disabled.

Message Lists.

Shortcut	Action
Up/Down	Highlight the next message up or down
Enter	Open a message
Spacebar	Check or uncheck a message's checkbox
Ctrl+Up/Down	Move focus up or down the list (preserving selection)
Ctrl+A	Select all messages
V	Toggle Preview Pane

General Commands.

Shortcut	Action
Delete	Sends the selected messages to the Trash.
E	Archives the selected messages.
M	Check mail (jumps to Inbox)
Shift+M	Check all mail (includes POP accounts)
N	Start a new email message
Ctrl+Shift+M	Start a new Instant Message (IM)
Ctrl+Shift+Y	Start a new SMS message (text)
Esc	Close the current tab
[	Move to the previous tab
]	Move to the next tab
S	Search
Semicolon	Open Settings
Ctrl+Shift+S	Activate voice commands
Ctrl+Shift+X	Deactivate voice commands

Compose.

Shortcut	Action
Ctrl+Shift+U	Attach files (one at a time)
Ctrl+S	Save as a draft
Ctrl+Enter	Send message
Ctrl+U	Underline
Ctrl+B	Bold
Ctrl+I	Italics
Alt+Shift+5	Strikethrough
Ctrl+Shift+E	Center text

Ctrl+Shift+L	Align Left
Ctrl+Shift+R	Align Right

Messages.

Shortcut	Action
R	Reply to a message
A	Reply all to a message
F	Forward a message
K	Mark as read/unread
L	Star/Unstar a message
P	Print message
Delete	Delete message
Shift+C	Add sender to contacts
D	Open Move menu
D then 1-9	Move message (s) to one of your first 9 folders
D then Ctrl+Shift+E	Move message (s) to a new folder
Ctrl+Shift+E	Create a new folder
[left arrow]	Previous message
[right arrow]	Next message

Attachment Previews.

Shortcut	Action
[left arrow]	Previous attachment
[right arrow]	Next attachment
Up/Down	Scroll through an attachment

Ctrl+F	Switches to expanded view from side by side mode
Esc	Returns to previous mode
Ctrl+[++]	Zooms in on a document
Ctrl+[--]	Zooms out on a document

CHAPTER 5.

Tips, Tricks, Techniques, and Keyboard Shortcuts for use in Fastmail.

Introduction: FastMail is an email service offering paid email accounts for individuals and organizations which is available in 36 languages. The company is FastMail Pty Ltd of Melbourne, Victoria, Australia. In 2010 the company was acquired by Opera Software.

-Wikipedia

A fresh topic

Features of FastMail.

Here are some features Fastmail has.

Access Messages.

FastMail provides a number of ways to access your email. Whether you're at home, the office, or an internet cafe,

FastMail allows you to view, send, and reply to messages, or upload and publish files to your own domain.

- Use their mobile app from your phone or tablet.
- Use their powerful custom web interface for accessing all your mail features.
- Access and send email with common tools like Outlook or Mail.app through IMAP or POP and SMTP.
- Let FastMail travel with you on your phone or tablet using their app.
- Manage and access your address book(s) everywhere using CardDAV.
- Access files with Windows Explorer, Mac Finder etc. through FTP or WebDAV.
- Every feature includes SSL support to ensure security.
- Publish files to personal websites, such as http://yourname.fastmail.com or http://yourdomain.com.
- Publish files as instant photo galleries (Like this sample).

Receive Messages

FastMail can provide a number of aliases for you to receive email, and domains to make your correspondence more professional and memorable. Powerful filters can help keep out unwanted mail and organise your messages with ease.

- Retrieve mail from other accounts, including Gmail, Yahoo! Mail, or Outlook.

- Sub-domain and plus-addressing keep track of separate email addresses.
- Multiple email addresses/aliases can be used to receive mail.
- Choose from many domains or use your own.
- Use simple and powerful DNS controls to maintain your domain.
- Filter mail with their powerful interface or scriptable sieve.
- File mail into a nearly unlimited hierarchical structure.

Filter Spam.

Fastmail advanced broad-spectrum spam filters sift out useless and potentially dangerous messages. They use techniques to detect, block and destroy spam- and virus-emitting bots. A system of smart and constantly updated greylists stop spambots without delaying legitimate email. And, they reference a high-quality DNS-based blackhole list to flag and reject messages from known spammers.

Fastmail protects your inbox from backscatter, preventing unsolicited bulk emails from reaching you. They analyze message headers and make sure your incoming mail is from trusted parties. Their servers parse incoming messages to detect common forms of spam and links to known spam sites.

Your personal spam filters can be trained and will get better at identifying and rejecting spam over time.

Block Viruses

Nigerian princes, long-lost relatives, and all sorts of other trojan horses are no match for FastMail's advanced virus filters. FastMail constantly finds and keeps up-to-date with the latest threats on the web, giving you the confidence to open mail without worrying about malware of fraudulent material.

Fastmail spambot detection and filtering means that >90% of virus threats never even enter the system of Fastmail in the first place. They support a product with the fastest response time to new threats of any and all virus protectors.

Don't fall for the claims of anti-virus software vendors. They specialise in anti-virus software running on Windows machines, not in detecting viruses in emails.

Manage Your Contacts.

FastMail organises your contacts, and can recall them with only a few clues from you. The service supports a number of importing options to allow you upload contact information from your home and work devices. Or you can keep your contacts in sync with your phone, tablet and desktop using CardDAV.

Organise Your Calendar.

FastMail provides a powerful calendar that lets you organise your life. Stay up to date by syncing your calendar with your phone, tablet and PC using CalDAV. Coordinate easily with shared calendars, or quickly email out invites. Comprehensive time zone support for globe trotters. Precise controls allow you to share what you want, and keep your private events private. Easily add public calendars from the internet, such as national holidays. Make changes fast with Fastmail's beautiful and intuitive drag 'n' drop interface.

Check Your Mail from any Browser

You can easily access your email from any computer or phone that has an internet connection. Their webmail interface is designed for speed and usability on all devices of any screen size.

End of Topic.

A fresh topic

Keyboard Shortcuts in Fastmail.

Keyboard shortcuts allow you to quickly perform an action without removing your hands from the keyboard to use your mouse or touchpad. If a button has a keyboard shortcut, you can quickly find it by hovering your mouse over the button. A tooltip will display with the shortcut key.

Use the following list of keyboard shortcuts to enhance your productivity in Fastmail.

Global Navigation.

Switch to another app or screen within FastMail with these keyboard shortcuts:

Shortcut	Action	Description
Shift+G then M	Mail	Go your mail.
Shift+G then A	Address Book	Go your contacts.
Shift+G then C	Calendar	Go your calendar.
Shift+G then N	Notes	Go your notes.
Shift+G then F	Files	Go your file storage.
Shift+G then B	Billing & Plan	Mange your account subscription and plan.
Shift+G then S	Settings	Open the settings for your account.
Shift+G then?	Help	Open the FastMail help.
Shift+G then L	Log out	Log out of your account.

Mail Shortcuts.

These commands will work when you are viewing message lists in your Inbox or other folders.

General mail actions

Shortcut	Action	Description
C	Compose	Start composing a new message.
G	Go to folder	Quickly switch to a folder. Type the first few characters of the folder name, or use the up/down arrow keys to move

		between the matching folders. If a folder name is more than one word, you can match either word. Press Enter to open the selected folder.
Z	Undo	Undo the last thing you did, if possible.
Space	Page down	Scroll down one page (window-height).
Shift+Space	Page up	Scroll up one page (window-height).
/	Search messages	Focus the mail search box. Searches all folders by default. Use Alt+Enter to limit to the current folder only, or Shift+Enter to force searching all folders.
Esc	Cancel	Remove focus from a text box.

Navigate, Refresh, Select & Pin.

These actions apply while viewing your mailbox list. The currently focussed conversation is shown in the mailbox list with a blue line to the left of the checkbox.

Shortcut	Action	Description
U	Refresh	Check for any new messages or other changes to your mail.
J	Focus next	Move the focus down one conversation.
K	Focus previous	Move the focus up one conversation.

O or Enter	Open	Display the currently focussed conversation.
X	Select or deselect	Toggle the selection of the currently focussed conversation so you can perform an action (see next section).
S	Toggle pinned	Toggles the pinned status of the currently focussed conversation or message.
Shift+X	Select/deselect a range	Toggle the selection of the currently focussed conversation, and also set the same selections state on all conversations between the focussed conversation and the last conversation on which you changed selection.
* then A or ' then A	Select all	Select **all conversations in the mailbox**.
* then N or ' then N	Unselect all	Clear any current selection.

Conversation Actions

When viewing your mailbox list, these actions apply to any selected conversations. Selected messages appear with a checkmark to the left and are highlighted in a different colour. When reading a conversation, these actions apply just to that conversation.

Shortcut	**Action**	**Description**

D or # or Delete	Delete	Move every message in the selected conversations to your Trash folder. If they are already in the Trash folder, this will **delete the messages permanently** instead.
M	Move	Move the selected conversations to a different folder. Type the first few characters of the folder name, or use the up/down arrow keys to move between the matching folders. If a folder name is more than one word, you can match either word. Press Enter to move the conversations to the selected folder.
Y	Archive	Mark the selected conversations as read and move them to the Archive folder.
!	Report spam	Train your spam filter to recognise the selected conversations as spam, and move them to your Spam folder.
. then r	Mark read	Mark all messages in the selected conversations as read.
. then u	Mark unread	Mark all messages in the selected conversation as unread.

. then p	Pin	Pin the selected conversations.
. then n	Unpin	Remove the pin from the selected conversations.
%	Permanently delete	Delete the selected conversations forevever **(cannot be undone)**.

Message Actions.

While reading a conversation, the following additional shortcuts are available.

Shortcut	Action	Description
J	Next	Open the next conversation down in the mailbox list.
K	Previous	Open the previous conversation in the mailbox list.
U	Return to the mailbox list.	
R	Reply	Start a new reply to the sender or mailing list of the last message in the conversation (depending on whether the message came from a mailing list).
A	Reply to all	Start a new reply to all the participants in the last message of the conversation.
Alt+R	Reply to sender	Start a new reply to just the sender of the last message in the conversation, even if the Reply-

		to header is set to reply back to a mailing list.
F	Forward	Forward the last message in the conversation to someone else.
Shift+L	Display images	If the conversation has messages with blocked images, display them.
Shift+E	Expand all	Expand all collapsed messages in the conversation.
N	Focus next	Focus and scroll to the next message in the conversation. A focussed message is shown with a blue line to the left of the avatar at the top. When a message is focussed, the R/A/Alt+R/F shortcuts apply to that message instead of the last message in the conversation.
P	Focus previous	Focus and scroll to the previous message in the conversation. A focussed message is shown with a blue line to the left of the avatar at the top. When a message is focussed, the R/A/Alt+R/F shortcuts apply to that message instead of the last message in the conversation.
E	Expand	Expand or collapse the currently focussed message.
;	More actions	Show the "More actions" menu for the currently focussed message. You can then use the arrow keys and Enter to select an action. Note, the message must

		be expanded for this shortcut to be applicable.
:	Toggle message details	Show or hide the message details for the currently focussed message.
"	toggle quotes	Show or hide all collapsed quotes in the currently focussed message.

Compose Shortcuts.

The following shortcuts can be used while composing messages.

Shortcut	Action	Description
Ctrl+Enter	Send	Send the message.
Ctrl+S	Save draft	Save the message to the Drafts folder.
Ctrl+Shift+Alt+Backspace	Discard	Discard the message and any saved draft.
Ctrl+Shift+C	Show Cc	Shows the Cc field, if hidden.
Ctrl+Shift+B	Show Bcc	Shows the Bcc field, if hidden.
Ctrl+M	Format text	This only applies when

		in **plain text** mode. Rewraps paragraphs and tries to align text to make it neater.
Ctrl+B	Bold	Toggle bold in rich text.
Ctrl+I	Italic	Toggle italic in rich text.
Ctrl+U	Underline	Toggle underline in rich text.
Ctrl+Shift+5	Subscript	Toggle subscript in rich text.
Ctrl+Shift+6	Superscript	Toggle superscript in rich text.
Ctrl+Shift+7	Strikethroug h	Toggle strikethroug h in rich text.
Ctrl+Shift+8	Bullet list	Make a bullet list.
Ctrl+Shift+9	Numbered list	Make a numbered list.
Tab (at start of list item)	Indent list	Increase the indent level of the list. Note, this

		shortcut is only active when the cursor is at the **beginning** of a list item.
Shift+Tab (at start of list item)	Unindent list	Decrease the indent level of the list. Note, this shortcut is only active when the cursor is at the **beginning** of a list item.
Ctrl+[	Remove quote	Decrease the quote level.
Ctrl+]	Add quote	Increase the quote level.

Address Book Shortcuts.

The following shortcuts can be used while viewing your address book.

Shortcut	Action	Description
N	New contact	Create a new contact.
J	Next	Focus and show the next contact.

K	Previous	Focus and show the previous contact.
X	Select/deselect	Select or deselect the focussed contact.
S	Toggle pinned	Toggles the pinned status of the focussed contact.
Shift+X	Select/deselect a range	Toggle the selection of the currently focussed contact, and also set the same selections state on all contacts between the focussed contact and the last contact on which you changed selection.
E	Edit	Edit the focussed contact.
Ctrl+S	Save	Save any changes you've made to the contact you are editing.
Esc	Discard changes	Stop editing and discard any changes you made.
# or Delete	Delete	Delete the selected contacts.
R	Groups	Add or remove the selected contacts to/from a contact group.
/	Search	Focus the contacts search box.
Z	Undo	Undo the last thing you did, if possible.

Calendar Shortcuts.

The following shortcuts can be used while viewing your calendar.

Shortcut	Action	Description
N	New event	Create a new event.
Alt	Copy event	Holding alt down while dragging an event will make a copy of the event instead of moving it.
C	Calendars	Show the menu for toggling visibility of calendars on and off.
V	Switch view	Flip between Overview and Detail view.
O	Time zone	Change the time zone in which the calendar is viewed (to use this, first enable multiple time zone support in the settings).
G	Go to date	Type in a date and hit enter to quickly jump to a specific date. The input accepts most date formats.
T	Go to today	Quickly jump to today in the current view.
J	Next	Move the view forward one week (overview) or day (detail view).
K	Previous	Move the view back one week (overview) or day (detail view).

Ctrl+S	Save	Save any changes you've made to the event you are editing.
Esc	Close pop over	Closes any pop over currently visible.
Z or Ctrl+Z	Undo	Undo the last thing you did. You can undo up to your last 10 previous actions.
Ctrl+Shift+Z	Redo	Redo the last thing you undid.

Notes Shortcuts.

The following shortcuts can be used while viewing your notes.

Shortcut	Action	Description
N	New note	Create a new note.
J	Next	Show the next note.
K	Previous	Show the previous note.
S	Toggle pinned	Toggles the pinned status of the focussed note.
E	Edit	Edit the visible note.
Ctrl+S	Save	Save any changes you've made to the note you are editing.
Esc	Discard changes	Stop editing and discard any changes you made.
# or Delete	Delete	Delete the visible note.
/	Search	Focus the notes search box.
Z	Undo	Undo the last thing you did, if possible.

CHAPTER 6.

Tips, Tricks, Techniques, and Keyboard Shortcuts for use in icloud Mail.

Introduction: This is an email service provided by Apple Inc. to their customers or subscribers. Having an icloud email account provides their customers with 5GB storage space for their mail.

A fresh topic

Manually Configuring an iCloud Email Account.

By Christopher Breen - Senior Editor.

Reader Matthew Hansman and his iCloud account need to come to a more mutually satisfactory understanding. He writes:

Some people have had some difficulty making older MobileMe accounts work with iCloud. And yet when they try to manually set up such an account, they're thwarted because there doesn't appear to be a way to fiddle with iCloud's IMAP and SMTP settings. But you can if you know the secret.

And here's that secret. While in Mail's Accounts setting, click on the Plus button and enter your iCloud address and password as you normally would. The button at the bottom will read Create. Hold down the Option key and that button changes to read Continue. Click on Continue. Instead of your account being set up for you, you can now set it up manually.

In the next sheet (which reads Incoming Mail Server), choose IMAP from the Account Type pop-up menu. Leave iCloud in the description field. In the Incoming Mail Server field enter *imap.mail.me.com.* Your user name and password should be filled in automatically. If the button at the bottom of the sheet doesn't read Continue, hold down the Option key and it will. Click that button.

Holding down the Option key allows you to manually configure an iCloud email account

In the next sheet (Incoming Mail Security) enable the Use Secure Socket Layer (SSL) option and choose Password from the Authentication pop-up menu. Click Continue (again, holding down the Option key if the button reads Create).

In the Outgoing Mail Server sheet that now appears, enter *iCloud* in the Description field, enter *smtp.mail.me.com* in the Outgoing Mail Server field, enable the Use Authentication option, and enter your complete email address in the User Name field and password in the Password field. Click Continue.

In the penultimate Outgoing Mail Security sheet enable the Use Secure Sockets Layer (SSL) option and, from the Authentication pop-up menu, be sure Password is selected. Click Continue again.

The final sheet will show you the account configuration. Look it over to make sure everything is entered correctly. (If it isn't, use the Go Back button to do exactly that and make corrections where needed.) Now click Create to create your account. Your email account should now work as expected.

End of Topic.

A fresh topic ⌐↳

Five iCloud Email Tricks you Probably Missed.

By Kirk McElhearn - Senior Contributor.

If you have an Apple ID, then you have an iCloud email account. This free account gives you up to 5GB storage for your emails, minus what you use for documents and other data you store in the cloud. It's easy to work with your iCloud email from Apple's Mail, on the Mac, or on an iOS device. Still, you may not know about the many extra options and features available if you log into iCloud on the Web.

Before you can take advantage of any of the following tips, you need to turn on iCloud. If you already have an Apple ID, which you use on the iTunes store, you may never have set up iCloud.. Once you've done that, you can use your email account and these five tricks.

1. Access email anywhere

While you may check your email on your Mac, iPhone or iPad, you can also access your messages on the Web. This is useful if you need to get or send email from a shared computer, but also if you need to send or receive files when you're on the road. Just log into icloud.com, and click the Mail icon. You'll have access to all of your email—and all of your contacts, if you've set iCloud to sync them—so you can send and receive messages and files. This can be useful if you need to get a file and print it out when you're visiting a client or friend.

2. Create rules that work on all your devices

You can set up rules—filters that act on incoming email messages—using Mail for OS X. But these rules only work on your Mac; they don't have any effect on your iPhone or iPad, unless you leave your Mac on all the time. If your Mac's not running, your email will simply flow into your iCloud account's inbox.

But you can set up rules on the icloud.com website that will move messages before they get to any of your devices. For example, you can filter your email so all the messages from your employer go into a specific mailbox.

To do this, you need to create a new mailbox; you can do this on your Mac or iOS device, but with iCloud on the Web, just click the plus-sign (+) icon next to Folders, then type a name for the new mailbox.

Next, click the gear icon at the top-right of the iCloud Mail interface, and choose *Rules*. Click *Add a Rule*, then choose one of the first conditions: if a message is from a specific person, has a subject containing a specific word, and so on. In the next field, enter an email address (for a specific person), a domain name, such as macworld.com (this will filter any messages from that domain), one or more words for subject filtering, and so on.

In the next section, choose either *Move to Folder, Move to Trash,* or *Forward to.* Then select the folder to move the message to, or the email address to forward it to. Click *Done*, and the rule will become active.

You can create rules so the iCloud sever will act on your email before it gets to your Mac or your iOS device.

Now, any messages meeting these conditions will be filtered on the iCloud server, and you won't need to leave your Mac on to do the job.

3. Let everyone know you're away.

Here's something you can't do in Mail on the Mac, or on iOS. If you're away from work, or on vacation, you may want to set up an auto-response to tell people when you'll be back. Click the gear icon at the top-right of the iCloud Mail page, then click *Preferences*. Click the *Vacation* icon, and check *Automatically reply to messages when they are received*. Enter the text you'd like sent, and then click *Done*.

You can combine this with Rules to route work messages to colleagues, too. After you've set up the auto-response, click *Rules*, and create a rule for specific addresses or domains, and forward them to the person at work who's filling in for you while you're away. When you get back from your trip, just delete the rule.

4. Forward emails to another account.

You probably don't have just an iCloud account; you may have another account for work as well. If you get some emails in your iCloud account, you can choose to forward them all to another account. This is a good way to use your iCloud account for some of your email, and download it when you check your main email account. Instead of checking two accounts, you can just check one.

Click the gear icon at the top-right of the iCloud Mail page, click *Preferences*, and then click *General*. Next to *Forwarding*, check *Forward my email to*, and enter an email address, such as your other account. You can also check *Delete messages after forwarding*, if you don't want them clogging up your iCloud mailbox.

5. Avoid spam with iCloud aliases.

Set up email aliases to protect your main address from spam. Use an alias to sign up for online newsletters, for example, or to post on message boards.

While you only have one iCloud email account, you can set up aliases or other addresses that you can use to send and receive emails with that account. In the iCloud email preferences, click *Accounts*, then, below the account list, click *Add an alias*. You can choose up to three aliases, and you may want to create one to use for online shopping sites, and another for friends, so you only use your main account for work. To avoid getting spam to your main address, use an alias when you have to give an email address to register.

The *Create Mail Alias* dialog box lets you choose an alias and apply a label to it. If the alias you want is taken, you'll be told that it's not available. Click *OK* to save the alias; you can then use it to send or receive email.

End of Topic.

A fresh topic

How to Set an Out of Office Automatic Reply Email Message for Outlook, iCloud, Gmail, and More.

By Jim Karpen.

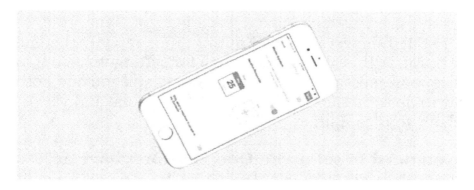

When you go on vacation, setting up an out of office (or OOO for short) message reply for incoming emails is an easy way to avoid your inbox without leaving people in the dark as to why you haven't responded. We wanted to cover setting up an out of office automatic reply across all the popular platforms from Outlook to Gmail. Most email providers require that out of office replies be set up on your computer. However, Gmail out of office reply allows you to set up ooo reply with the Gmail app on iPhone or iPad. If you have Verizon, you can even set up an out of office text message while you're gone too. We'll cover each in our walkthrough. Here's how to set up an out of office automatic reply email message for Outlook, iCloud, Gmail, and more.

There's a good reason most providers don't allow you to set up out of office reply in the apps on your iPhone or iPad. The change is usually done at the server level so that your email doesn't get stuck in an infinite loop. For example, if you and a friend both set up an automated reply by creating a rule in your desktop email programs, you could end up sending thousands of emails to each other, with each person's computer responding to the repeated out-of-office replies with its own out-of-office replies.

As I stated, however, Gmail out of office reply is the one exception to this. Our walkthrough for setting up an out of office mail message for Gmail accounts will include both how to do so in the Gmail app on your iPhone and via the web on your computer.

If you need to set up an Ooo but don't have access to a computer, you can use the Safari browser on your iPhone to visit your email provider. Just make sure you use the desktop version of the website by tapping the share icon and selecting Request Desktop Site. I also noticed while testing this that sometimes the screen was cut off, preventing me from completing my out of office reply. But if you're without a computer, this is the best mobile option.

If you use the iPhone & Mac Mail app to connect all of your accounts, you can set up an out of office reply directly within the OS X Mail app instead of having to set up ooo for all of your separate email accounts.

We'll cover how to turn off out of office reply for each mail provider as well. Let's get to it.

How to Set Up Email Auto Reply for iCloud Mail.

- Log-in to icloud.com.

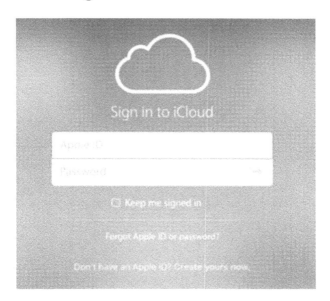

- Select Mail.

- Tap the Settings icon that looks like a gear in the bottom left corner.
- Select Preferences.

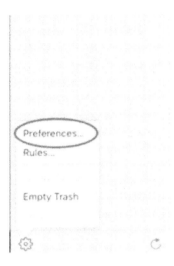

- Choose the Vacation tab at the top.
- Check the box that says, "Automatically reply to messages when they are received."
- Type your auto reply email message in the box below.
- Click Done.

When your vacation is over and you've returned, turn off out of office reply for iCloud by unchecking the "Automatically reply to messages..." box.

How to Set Up Out of Office Automatic Reply for Gmail.

In the Gmail App:

Gmail makes it particularly easy to setup your out of office reply. Simply,

- Open the Gmail app on your iPhone.
- Tap the three horizontal bars in the top left corner.
- Select the Settings icon that looks like a gear.
- Toggle On Vacation Responder.

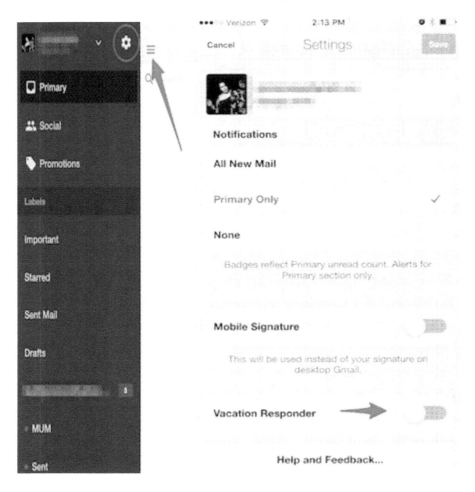

- Select your start and end date.
- Then type your auto email's subject and message.
- You can also choose to toggle on, "only send a response to people in my Contacts," if preferred.
- Tap Save at the top and you're done!

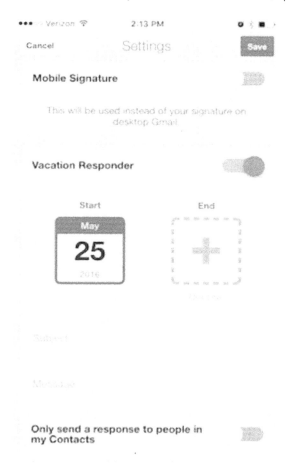

If you set an End date, the out of office reply will automatically turn off. If not, visit Settings in the Gmail app and toggle off Vacation Responder, then tap Save.

On Gmail.com:

- Log-in to Gmail.com.

- Tap the Settings icon that looks like a gear in the upper right corner.
- Choose Settings.

- Scroll down until you see Vacation Responder.
- Check the box Vacation responder on.
- Choose your start and (optional) end date.
- Enter your auto reply email's subject line and the message.
- There's an optional box you can check for sending the auto-reply email to only people in your contacts, if preferred.

- Click Save Changes.

If you set an end date, your out of office reply will automatically turn off. If not, you can follow the same steps to settings and check the box, "Vacation Responder off." Then save the changes.

How to Set Up Out of Office Automatic Reply for Outlook.

- Sign in to Outlook.com.
- Tap the Settings icon that looks like a gear in the top right corner.
- Choose Automatic Replies.

- Check the box Send Automatic Replies.
- Choose the start and end date, then check the box Send replies only during this time period.
- Below that is a blank body of text. Enter the message you want people to receive as your out of office reply.
- You can check the box for sending Ooo replies to everyone or just to your contacts.
- Click Ok at the top when you're done.

If you set a start and end time and check the box, "Send replies only during this time period," your out of office reply will automatically turn off. If not, you can easily turn off by revisiting settings, clicking Automatic Replies, and checking the box, "Don't send automatic replies."

How to Set Up Out of Office Response Email for Yahoo.

- Log-in to Yahoo.com.
- Click the Settings icon that looks like a gear in the top right corner.
- Select Settings.

- Choose Vacation Response.
- Check Enable during these dates.
- Set your dates.
- Below that, enter your auto reply email message.

- You can also send yourself a sample copy and set different responses for emails coming from specific domains.
- When you're done, click Save.

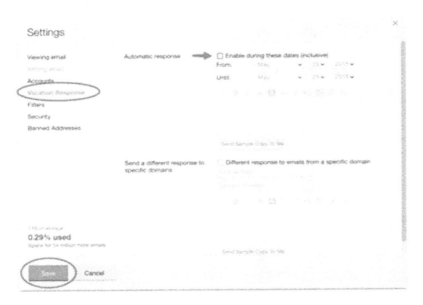

Your out of office vacation response should turn off automatically after the end date. But you can also revisit this place in Settings to turn it off manually by unchecking the box, "Enable during these dates," and clicking Save.

How to Set Up Automatic Email Reply for OS X Mail App.

If you manage all your accounts from the Mail app on iPhone and Mac, then you can create a "rule" that will work as your out of office automatic email response. It's not as straight-forward as going direct to the email provider, but it will do the job all the same and save you from having to set up multiple out of office replies for each of your email accounts. Here's how:

- Open the Mail app on your Mac.
- Click Mail on the top menu bar and select Preferences.

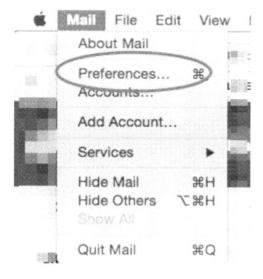

- Choose Rules.
- Select Add Rule.

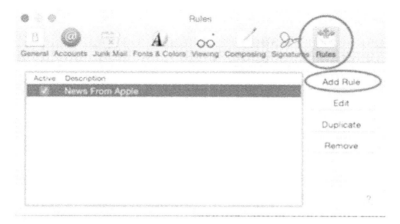

- Give it a description such as Out of Office Response.
- Where the default is Any Recipient, click and choose Every Message.
- Below that, change Move Message to Reply to Message.
- Click Reply Message text...

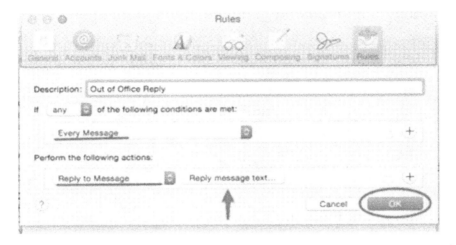

- Enter the email response you want people to see when they receive your Out of Office reply. Click Ok.

- Click Ok again to finish creating the rule.
- **This is where it gets tricky**:
- It will ask if you want to apply your rules to messages in selected inboxes. Choose **Don't Apply.** I repeat, choose **Don't Apply.** (If you choose Apply, every person in your inbox will receive your out of office reply. By choosing Don't Apply, only new messages will receive the out of office response.)

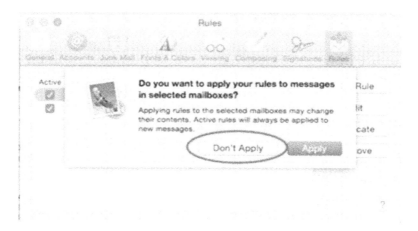

To send out of office replies to specific emails only:

- Follow the directions above until you come Every Message. Instead of Every Message, choose To.
- In the next box, choose "is equal to" and enter your email address for the account you want to send out of office replies to.
- If you need to set it up for more than one email address, click the plus sign and repeat.

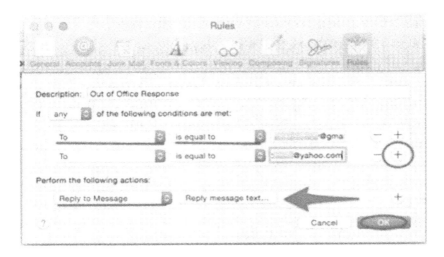

- Then continue as per the directions above.

To turn off this out of office reply, you'll need to open Preference up again, select Rules, and uncheck your Out of Office Response rule.

How to Set Up Automatic Responses for Text Messages.

Currently, this only works if your carrier is Verizon. To do this,

- Open the App Store on your iPhone.
- Download Verizon Messages+
- Upon opening the app, you'll have to enter your number. You'll then receive a confirmation code to enter. This will log you in.
- Tap the three horizontal bars in top left corner.
- Select Auto Reply.

- Choose Add a new message and write the automatic text response you want to send.
- Toggle Auto Reply On at the top.
- Set a date at the bottom under Until. The auto reply will turn off on the day you select.
- Tap Done.

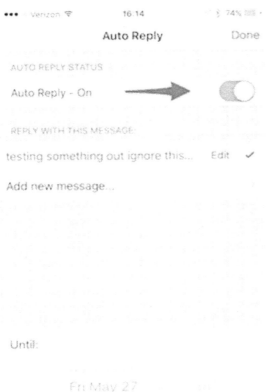

Your auto response text message will turn off automatically on the day selected. Or you can navigate to the same place within the app and toggle Auto Reply off at any time.

End of Topic.

A fresh topic ⌐
└▶

Email Keyboard Shortcuts in iCloud

You can use your keyboard to quickly accomplish many tasks in iCloud Mail. To complete an action using a Mac or a Windows computer, press the keys listed below.

Action	Mac Shortcut	Windows Shortcut
Archive an email message	Command–Down Arrow	Control–Down Arrow
Bold	Command-B	Control-B
Compose a new email message	Option-Shift-N	Alt-Shift-N
Delete a selected message or folder	Delete	Backspace
Flag or unflag email	Shift-Command-L	Control-Shift-L
Indent items in a list	Command–Right Bracket	Control–Right Bracket
Italic	Command-I	Control-I
Make font size bigger	Command–Equal Sign	Control–Equal Sign
Make font size smaller	Command–Minus Sign	Control–Minus Sign
Mark email as Junk or Not Junk	Shift-Command-J	Control-Shift-J
Mark email as Read or Unread	Shift-Command-U	Control-Shift-U
Open the selected message in a new window	Return	Return

Outdent items in a list	Command–Left Bracket	Control–Left Bracket
Print	Command-P	Control-P
Redo changes to an email message	Shift-Command-Z	Control-Shift-Z
Reply to sender	Shift-Command-R	Control-Shift-R
Save as a draft	Command-S	Control-S
Scroll through the selected messages	Space bar	Space
Select all email messages	Command-A	Control-A
Send email message	Shift-Command-D	Control-Shift-D
Toggle between Reply and Reply All	Shift-Command-R	Control-Shift-R
Underline	Command-U	Control-U
Undo changes to an email message	Command-Z	Control-Z

CHAPTER 7.

Tips, Tricks, Techniques, and Keyboard Shortcuts for use in Outlook Mail.

Introduction: Microsoft Outlook is an application designed by Microsoft Corporation that keeps people connected through its email services, and other powerful organizational tools.

A fresh topic

Security Features in Outlook.

Security features in Outlook.com (formerly Hotmail) can help protect you from spam and fraud.

Sign in with your Microsoft account.

Use your <u>Microsoft account</u>—a single email address and password—to sign in to Outlook. You also use your Microsoft account to sign into any device running Windows 8 or Windows RT and to other Microsoft services like Messenger, Xbox LIVE, and OneDrive.

Call us overprotective.

To help protect your personal data, we (Microsoft team) ask everyone who has a Microsoft account to make sure that the security information associated with their account is correct and up to date. When your security information (like an alternate email address or phone number) is current, we (Microsoft team) can use it to verify your identity if there's ever a problem. For example, if you forget your password, or if someone else tries to take over your account, Microsoft uses your security details to help you get back into your account.

If you see a message asking you to update or verify your Microsoft account security information, you have seven days to do it.

Get rid of spam.

Outlook uses Microsoft SmartScreen—the same technology that businesses and governments use to help protect their employee email. SmartScreen works mostly behind the scenes to separate legitimate messages from spam and help keep your inbox free of scams.

When you receive email from a sender that Microsoft has verified, the trusted sender icon appears next to the message. The trusted sender icon is a green shield with a check mark. This icon helps you determine if a message comes from a legitimate sender such as your bank.

If you trust the person or website that sent you a message, you can mark them as safe. This sends any messages from them straight to your inbox.

Spammers sometimes use automated programs to create Outlook or other email accounts and then send junk email from them. That's why Microsoft will periodically prompt you to verify your account.

Watch for yellow and red safety bars.

Outlook automatically verifies senders and use a safety bar within an email message to warn you about potentially harmful senders.

A yellow safety bar in your email message means that the message contains blocked attachments, pictures, or links to websites. If you don't recognize and trust the sender of the message, don't download any attachments or pictures and don't click any links in the message.

A red safety bar in an email message means that the message you received contains something that might be unsafe and has been blocked by Outlook. We recommend deleting these types of email messages from your inbox without opening them.

Connect with HTTPS.

HTTPS (Hypertext Transfer Protocol Secure) helps protect information that's sent over the Internet. Outlook always uses HTTPS to encrypt your sign-in information (email address and password). When you sign in to your Outlook account, you have extra security when you read or write email.

HTTPS helps keep your account secure from hackers, especially if you commonly use public computers or unsecure wireless connections.

Keep your email address private.

If you don't want to give your personal email address to online retailers or others who might send unwanted email, you can create another email address (an "alias") within your account. When someone sends an email to your alias, it goes to a folder in Outlook that you designate. When you're done with the alias, you can delete it.

When you use an alias, people will not know your real email address. This means less spam and more privacy.

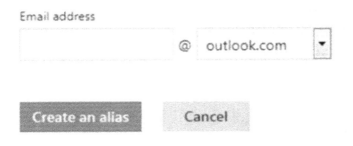

With Outlook you can create up to five email aliases within your account each year. You can create a different alias for each aspect of your online life. For example, you might have one alias for gaming, one for communicating with old friends, and one for your work life.

Help your hacked friends

If cybercriminals hack into an account, they can use the hacked person's contact list (often the first people to know that an account has been compromised) to send unwanted or even dangerous spam messages. This spam appears to originate from a trusted source, but it can contain malicious links or fake stories about how the sender is in danger and needs money right away.

If you get mail like this, you can use a feature in Outlook to report that someone else's account has been hacked. You can even use this feature for messages from people who use other email providers.

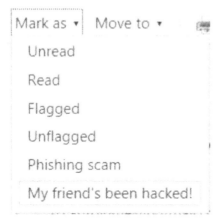

Be safer when you use a public computer.

Each time you use your Microsoft account to sign in to webmail from a public computer (like those at airports, coffee shops, and Internet cafes), you can request a single-use code. You use the code only once and avoid typing your real password to sign in to a computer that might be controlled by a cybercriminal.

On the Outlook sign-in page, click **Sign in with a single-use code,** and Microsoft will send a one-time use authentication code to a mobile phone or another email address that you've already given them.

End of Topic.

A fresh topic

Keyboard Shortcut in Outlook 2016 for Windows.

Use the following list of keyboard shortcuts to enhance your productivity in Microsoft Outlook.

Keyboard Shortcuts For SmartArt Graphics.

Insert a SmartArt graphic in an Office document

1. In the Microsoft Office program where you want to insert the graphic, press Alt, then N, and then M to open the **SmartArt Graphic** dialog box.
2. Press Up Arrow or Down Arrow to select the type of graphic that you want.
3. Press Tab to move to the Layout task pane.

4. Press the arrow keys to select the layout that you want.
5. Press Enter to insert the selected layout.

Work With Shapes In A SmartArt Graphic

Action	Shortcut
Select the next element in a SmartArt graphic.	Tab
Select the previous element in a SmartArt graphic.	Shift+Tab
Select all shapes.	Ctrl +A
Remove focus from the selected shape.	Esc
Nudge the selected shape up.	Up Arrow
Nudge the selected shape down.	Down Arrow
Nudge the selected shape left.	Left Arrow
Nudge the selected shape right.	Right Arrow
Edit text in the selected shape.	Enter or F2, Esc to exit shape
Delete the selected shape.	Delete or Backspace
Cut the selected shape.	Ctrl+X or Shift+Delete
Copy the selected shape.	Ctrl+C
Paste the contents of the Clipboard.	Ctrl+V
Undo the last action.	Ctrl+Z

Move And Resize Shapes In A SmartArt Graphic

Action	Shortcut
Enlarge the selected shape horizontally.	Shift+Right Arrow

Reduce the selected shape horizontally.	Shift+Left Arrow
Enlarge the selected shape vertically.	Shift+Up Arrow
Reduce the selected shape vertically.	Shift+Down Arrow
Rotate the selected shape to the right.	Alt+Right Arrow
Rotate the selected shape to the left.	Alt+Left Arrow

Notes:

- To apply more precise adjustments to shapes, press the Ctrl key in addition to any of the above keyboard shortcuts.
- These keyboard shortcuts apply to multiple selections as if you selected each item individually.

Work With Text In A SmartArt Graphic

Action	Shortcut
Move one character to the left.	Left Arrow
Move one character to the right.	Right Arrow
Move up one line.	Up Arrow
Move down one line.	Down Arrow
Move one word to the left.	Ctrl+Left Arrow
Move one word to the right.	Ctrl+Right Arrow
Move one paragraph up.	Ctrl+Up Arrow
Move one paragraph down.	Ctrl+Down Arrow
Move to the end of a line.	End
Move to the beginning of a line.	Home
Move to the end of a text box.	Ctrl+End

Move to the beginning of a text box.	Ctrl+Home
Cut selected text.	Ctrl+X
Copy selected text.	Ctrl+C
Paste selected text.	Ctrl+V
Move the selected text up.	Alt+Shift+Up Arrow
Move the selected text down.	Alt+Shift+Down Arrow
Undo the last action.	Ctrl+Z
Delete one character to the left.	Backspace
Delete one word to the left.	Ctrl+Backspace
Delete one character to the right.	Delete
Delete one word to the right.	Ctrl+Delete
Promote the selected text.	Alt+Shift+Left Arrow
Demote the selected text.	Alt+Shift+Right Arrow
Check the spelling (not available in Word).	F7

Apply Character Formatting

Action	Shortcut
Open the **Font** dialog box.	Ctrl+Shift+F or Ctrl+Shift+P
Increase the font size of the selected text.	Ctrl+Shift+>
Decrease the font size of the selected text.	Ctrl+Shift+<
Switch the case of selected text (lower case, Title Case, UPPER CASE).	Shift+F3
Apply bold formatting to the selected text.	Ctrl+B

Apply an underline to the selected text.	Ctrl+U
Apply italic formatting to the selected text.	Ctrl+I
Apply subscript formatting to the selected text.	Ctrl+Equal Sign
Apply superscript formatting to the selected text.	Ctrl+Shift+Plus Sign
Adjust the superscript/subscript offset up.	Ctrl+Alt+Shift+>
Adjust the superscript/subscript offset down.	Ctrl+Alt+Shift+<
Remove all character formatting from the selected text.	Shift+Ctrl+Spacebar

Copy Text Formatting

Action	Shortcut
Copy formatting from the selected text.	Shift+Ctrl+C
Paste formatting to the selected text.	Shift+Ctrl+V

Apply Paragraph Formatting

Action	Shortcut
Center a paragraph.	Ctrl+E
Justify a paragraph.	Ctrl+J
Left align a paragraph.	Ctrl+L
Right align a paragraph.	Ctrl+R
Demote a bullet point.	Tab or Alt+Shift+Right Arrow

Promote a bullet point.	Shift+Tab or Alt+Shift+Left Arrow

Use The Text Pane

Action	Shortcut
Merge two lines of text.	Delete at the end of the first line of text
Display the shortcut menu.	Shift+F10
Switch between the **Text** pane and the drawing canvas.	Ctrl+Shift+F2
Close the **Text** pane.	Alt+F4
Switch the focus from the **Text** pane to the border of the SmartArt graphic.	Esc
Open the SmartArt graphics Help topic. (Your pointer should be in the Text pane.)	Ctrl +Shift+F1

Use The Keyboard To Work With The Ribbon.

Do tasks quickly without using the mouse by pressing a few keys—no matter where you are in an Office program. You can get to every command on the ribbon by using an access key—usually by pressing two to four keys.

1. Press and release the ALT key.

   You see the little boxes called KeyTips over each command available in the current view.

2. Press the letter shown in the KeyTip over the command you want to use.

3. Depending on which letter you pressed, you might see additional KeyTips. For example, if the **Home** tab is active and you pressed N, the **Insert** tab is displayed, along with the KeyTips for the groups in that tab.
4. Continue pressing letters until you press the letter of the specific command you want to use.

Tip: To cancel the action you're taking and hide the KeyTips, press and release the ALT key.

Change the keyboard focus without using the mouse.

Another way to use the keyboard to work with the ribbon is to move the focus among the tabs and commands until you find the feature you want to use. The following shows some ways to move the keyboard focus without using the mouse.

Action	Shortcut
Select the active tab and show the access keys.	ALT or F10. Press either of these keys again to move back to the Office file and cancel the access keys.
Move to another tab.	ALT or F10 to select the active tab, and then LEFT ARROW or RIGHT ARROW.
Move to another Group on the active tab.	ALT or F10 to select the active tab, and then CTRL+RIGHT ARROW

	or LEFT ARROW to move between groups.
Minimize (collapse) or restore the ribbon.	CTRL+F1
Display the shortcut menu for the selected item.	SHIFT+F10
Move the focus to select the active tab, your Office file, task pane, or status bar.	F6
Move the focus to each command in the ribbon, forward or backward.	ALT or F10, and then TAB or SHIFT+TAB
Move down, up, left, or right among the items in the ribbon.	DOWN ARROW, UP ARROW, LEFT ARROW, or RIGHT ARROW
Go to the selected command or control in the ribbon.	SPACE BAR or ENTER
Open the selected menu or gallery in the ribbon.	SPACE BAR or ENTER
Go to a command or option in the ribbon so you can change it.	ENTER
Finish changing the value of a command or option in the ribbon, and move focus back to the Office file.	ENTER
Get help on the selected command or control in the ribbon. (If no Help article is associated with the selected command, the Help table of contents for that program is shown instead.)	F1

Basic Navigation

Action	Shortcut
Switch to Mail.	Ctrl+1
Switch to Calendar.	Ctrl+2
Switch to Contacts.	Ctrl+3
Switch to Tasks.	Ctrl+4
Switch to Notes.	Ctrl+5
Switch to Folder List in Folder Pane.	Ctrl+6
Switch to Shortcuts.	Ctrl+7
Switch to next message (with message open).	Ctrl+Period
Switch to previous message (with message open).	Ctrl+Comma
Move between the Folder Pane, the main Outlook window, the Reading Pane, and the To-Do Bar.	Ctrl+Shift+Tab or Shift+Tab
Move between the Outlook window, the smaller panes in the Folder Pane, the Reading Pane, and the sections in the To-Do Bar.	Tab
Move between the Outlook window, the smaller panes in the Folder Pane, the Reading Pane, and the sections in the To-Do Bar, and show the access keys in the Outlook ribbon.	F6
Move around message header lines in the Folder Pane or an open message.	Ctrl+Tab

Move around within the Folder Pane.	Arrow keys
Go to a different folder.	Ctrl+Y
Go to the Search box.	F3 or Ctrl+E
In the Reading Pane, go to the previous message.	Alt+Up Arrow or Ctrl+Comma or Alt+Page Up
In the Reading Pane, page down through text.	Spacebar
In the Reading Pane, page up through text.	Shift+Spacebar
Collapse or expand a group in the email message list.	Left Arrow or Right Arrow, respectively
Go back to previous view in main Outlook window.	Alt+B or Alt+Left Arrow
Go forward to next view in main Outlook window.	Alt+Right Arrow
Select the InfoBar and, if available, show the menu of commands.	Ctrl+Shift+W

Search.

Action	Shortcut
Find a message or other item.	Ctrl+E
Clear the search results.	Esc
Expand the search to include **All Mail Items**, **All Calendar Items**, or **All Contact Items**, depending on the module you are in.	Ctrl+Alt+A
Use **Advanced Find**.	Ctrl+Shift+F
Create a Search Folder.	Ctrl+Shift+P
Search for text within an open item.	F4

Find and replace text, symbols, or some formatting commands. Works in the **Reading Pane** on an open item.	Ctrl+H
Expand search to include items from the current folder.	Ctrl+Alt+K
Expand search to include subfolders.	Ctrl+Alt+Z

Common Commands.

Commands common to most views

Action	Shortcut
Save (except in Tasks).	Ctrl+S or Shift+F12
Save and close (except in Mail).	Alt+S
Save as (only in Mail).	F12
Undo.	Ctrl+Z or Alt+Backspace
Delete an item.	Ctrl+D
Print.	Ctrl+P
Copy an item.	Ctrl+Shift+Y
Move an item.	Ctrl+Shift+V
Check names.	Ctrl+K
Check spelling.	F7
Flag for follow-up.	Ctrl+Shift+G
Forward.	Ctrl+F
Send or post or invite all.	Alt+S
Enable editing in a field (except in Mail or Icon view).	F2
Left align text.	Ctrl+L
Center text.	Ctrl+E
Right align text.	Ctrl+R

Format text

Action	Shortcut
Display the **Format** menu.	Alt+O
Display the **Font** dialog box.	Ctrl+Shift+P
Switch case (with text selected).	Shift+F3
Format letters as small capitals.	Ctrl+Shift+K
Make letters bold.	Ctrl+B
Add bullets.	Ctrl+Shift+L
Make letters italic.	Ctrl+I
Increase indent.	Ctrl+T
Decrease indent.	Ctrl+Shift+T
Left align.	Ctrl+L
Center.	Ctrl+E
Underline.	Ctrl+U
Increase font size.	Ctrl+] or Ctrl+Shift+>
Decrease font size.	Ctrl+[or Ctrl+Shift+<
Cut.	Ctrl+X or Shift+Delete
Copy.	Ctrl+C or Ctrl+Insert **Note:** Ctrl+Insert is not available in the Reading Pane.
Paste.	Ctrl+V or Shift+Insert
Clear formatting.	Ctrl+Shift+Z or Ctrl+Spacebar
Delete the next word.	Ctrl+Shift+H
Stretch a paragraph to fit between the margins.	Ctrl+Shift+J
Apply styles.	Ctrl+Shift+S
Create a hanging indent.	Ctrl+T

Insert a hyperlink.	Ctrl+K
Left align a paragraph.	Ctrl+L
Right align a paragraph.	Ctrl+R
Reduce a hanging indent.	Ctrl+Shift+T
Remove paragraph formatting.	Ctrl+Q

Add links and edit URLs

Action	Shortcut
Edit a URL in the body of an item.	Hold down Ctrl and click the mouse button.
Insert a hyperlink.	Ctrl+K

Create an item or file

Action	Shortcut
Create an appointment.	Ctrl+Shift+A
Create a contact.	Ctrl+Shift+C
Create a contact group.	Ctrl+Shift+L
Create a fax.	Ctrl+Shift+X
Create a folder.	Ctrl+Shift+E
Create a meeting request.	Ctrl+Shift+Q
Create a message.	Ctrl+Shift+M
Create a note.	Ctrl+Shift+N
Create a Microsoft Office document.	Ctrl+Shift+H
Post to this folder.	Ctrl+Shift+S
Post a reply in this folder.	Ctrl+T
Create a Search Folder.	Ctrl+Shift+P
Create a task.	Ctrl+Shift+K
Create a task request.	Ctrl+Shift+U

Color Categories

TASK	SHORTCUT
Delete the selected category from the list in the Color Categories dialog box.	Alt+D

Flags

Action	Shortcut
Open the **Flag for Follow Up** dialog box to assign a flag.	Ctrl+Shift+G

Mail

Action	Shortcut
Switch to **Inbox**.	Ctrl+Shift+I
Switch to **Outbox**.	Ctrl+Shift+O
Choose the account from which to send a message.	Ctrl+Tab (with focus on the **To** box), and then Tab to the **Accounts** button
Check names.	Ctrl+K
Send.	Alt+S
Reply to a message.	Ctrl+R
Reply all to a message.	Ctrl+Shift+R
Reply with meeting request.	Ctrl+Alt+R
Forward a message.	Ctrl+F
Mark a message as not junk.	Ctrl+ Alt+J
Display blocked external content (in a message).	Ctrl+Shift+I
Post to a folder.	Ctrl+ Shift+S

Apply Normal style.	Ctrl+Shift+N
Check for new messages.	Ctrl+M or F9
Go to the previous message.	Up Arrow
Go to the next message.	Down Arrow
Create a message (when in Mail).	Ctrl+N
Create a message (from any Outlook view).	Ctrl+Shift+M
Open a received message.	Ctrl+O
Delete and Ignore a Conversation.	Ctrl+Shift+D
Open the Address Book.	Ctrl+Shift+B
Add a Quick Flag to an unopened message.	Insert
Display the **Flag for Follow Up** dialog box.	Ctrl+Shift+G
Mark as read.	Ctrl+Q
Mark as unread.	Ctrl+U
Open the Mail Tip in the selected message.	Ctrl+Shift+W
Find or replace.	F4
Find next.	Shift+F4
Send.	Ctrl+Enter
Print.	Ctrl+P
Forward.	Ctrl+F
Forward as attachment.	Ctrl+Alt+F
Show the properties for the selected item.	Alt+Enter
Create a multimedia message	Ctrl+Shift+U

Mark for Download.	Ctrl+Alt+M
Clear Mark for Download.	Ctrl+Alt+U
Display Send/Receive progress.	Ctrl+B (when a Send/Receive is in progress)

Calendar

Action	Shortcut
Create an appointment (when in Calendar).	Ctrl+N
Create an appointment (in any Outlook view).	Ctrl+Shift+A
Create a meeting request.	Ctrl+Shift+Q
Forward an appointment or meeting.	Ctrl+F
Reply to a meeting request with a message.	Ctrl+R
Reply All to a meeting request with a message.	Ctrl+Shift+R
Show 1 day in the calendar.	Alt+1
Show 2 days in the calendar.	Alt+2
Show 3 days in the calendar.	Alt+3
Show 4 days in the calendar.	Alt+4
Show 5 days in the calendar.	Alt+5
Show 6 days in the calendar.	Alt+6
Show 7 days in the calendar.	Alt+7
Show 8 days in the calendar.	Alt+8
Show 9 days in the calendar.	Alt+9
Show 10 days in the calendar.	Alt+0
Go to a date.	Ctrl+G
Switch to Month view.	Alt+= or Ctrl+Alt+4
Go to the next day.	Ctrl+Right Arrow

Go to the next week.	Alt+Down Arrow
Go to the next month.	Alt+Page Down
Go to the previous day.	Ctrl+Left Arrow
Go to the previous week.	Alt+Up Arrow
Go to the previous month.	Alt+Page Up
Go to the start of the week.	Alt+Home
Go to the end of the week.	Alt+End
Switch to Full Week view.	Alt+Minus Sign or Ctrl+Alt+3
Switch to Work Week view.	Ctrl+Alt+2
Go to previous appointment.	Ctrl+Comma or Ctrl+Shift+Comma
Go to next appointment.	Ctrl+Period or Ctrl+Shift+Period
Set up recurrence for an open appointment or meeting.	Ctrl+G

See also under Views, Calendar Day/Week/Month view, and Date Navigator.

People

Action	Shortcut
Dial a new call.	Ctrl+Shift+D
Find a contact or other item (Search).	F3 or Ctrl+E
Enter a name in the **Search Address Books** box.	F11
In Table or List view of contacts, go to first contact that starts with a specific letter.	Shift+letter
Select all contacts.	Ctrl+A

Create a message with selected contact as subject.	Ctrl+F
Create a contact (when in Contacts).	Ctrl+N
Create a contact (from any Outlook view).	Ctrl+Shift+C
Open a contact form for the selected contact.	Ctrl+O
Create a contact group.	Ctrl+Shift+L
Print.	Ctrl+P
Update a list of contact group members.	F5
Go to a different folder.	Ctrl+Y
Open the Address Book.	Ctrl+Shift+B
Use **Advanced Find**.	Ctrl+Shift+F
In an open contact, open the next contact listed.	Ctrl+Shift+Period
Find a contact.	F11
Close a contact.	ESC
Send a fax to the selected contact.	Ctrl+Shift+X
Open the **Check Address** dialog box.	Alt+D
In a contact form, under **Internet**, display the **Email 1** information.	Alt+Shift+1
In a contact form, under **Internet**, display the **Email 2** information.	Alt+Shift+2
In a contact form, under **Internet**, display the **Email 3** information.	Alt+Shift+3

Electronic Business Cards

Action	**Shortcut**
Open the **Add** list.	Alt+A

Select text in **Label** box when the field with a label assigned is selected.	Alt+B
Open the **Add Card Picture** dialog box.	Alt+C
Place cursor at beginning of **Edit** box.	Alt+E
Select the **Fields** box.	Alt+F
Select the **Image Align** drop-down list.	Alt+G
Select color palette for background.	Alt+K, then Enter
Select **Layout** drop-down list.	Alt+L
Remove a selected field from the **Fields** box.	Alt+R

Tasks

Action	Shortcut
Accept a task request.	Alt+C
Decline a task request.	Alt+D
Find a task or other item.	Ctrl+E
Open the **Go to Folder** dialog box.	Ctrl+Y
Create a task (when in Tasks).	Ctrl+N
Create a task (from any Outlook view).	Ctrl+Shift+K
Open selected item.	Ctrl+O
Print selected item.	Ctrl+P
Select all items.	Ctrl+A
Delete selected item.	Ctrl+D
Forward a task as an attachment.	Ctrl+F
Create a task request.	Ctrl+Shift+Alt+U
Switch between the **Folder Pane**, **Tasks** list, and **To-Do Bar**.	Tab or Shift+Tab
Undo last action.	Ctrl+Z
Flag an item or mark complete.	Insert

Groups

Action	Shortcut
Expand a single selected group.	Right Arrow
Collapse a single selected group.	Left Arrow
Select the previous group.	Up Arrow
Select the next group.	Down Arrow
Select the first group.	Home
Select the last group.	End
Select the first item on screen in an expanded group or the first item off screen to the right.	Right Arrow

Print

Action	Shortcut
Open **Print** tab in Backstage view.	Press Alt+F, and then press P
To print an item from an open window.	Alt+F, press P, and then press F and press 1
Open **Page Setup** from **Print Preview**.	Alt+S or Alt+U
To select a printer from **Print Preview**.	Alt+F, press P, and then press I
To **Define Print Styles**.	Alt+F, press P, and then press L
To open **Print Options**.	Alt+F, press P, and then press R

Send/Receive.

Action	Shortcut
Start a send/receive for all defined Send/Receive groups with **Include this group in Send/Receive (F9)** selected. This can include headers, full items, specified folders, items less than a specific size, or any combination that you define.	F9
Start a send/receive for the current folder, retrieving full items (header, item, and any attachments).	Shift+F9
Start a send/receive.	Ctrl+M
Define Send/Receive groups.	Ctrl+Alt+S

Macros

Action	Shortcut
Play macro.	Alt+F8

Table view

Action	Shortcut
Open an item.	Enter
Select all items.	Ctrl+A
Go to the item at the bottom of the screen.	Page Down
Go to the item at the top of the screen.	Page Up
Extend or reduce the selected items by one item.	Shift+Up Arrow or Shift+Down Arrow, respectively

Go to the next or previous item without extending the selection.	Ctrl+Up Arrow or Ctrl+Down Arrow, respectively
Select or cancel selection of the active item.	Ctrl+Spacebar

Business Cards view or Address Cards view

Action	Shortcut
Select a specific card in the list.	One or more letters of the name that the card is filed under or the name of the field that you are sorting by
Select the previous card.	Up Arrow
Select the next card.	Down Arrow
Select the first card in the list.	Home
Select the last card in the list.	End
Select the first card on the current page.	Page Up
Select the first card on the next page.	Page Down
Select the closest card in the next column.	Right Arrow
Select the closest card in the previous column.	Left Arrow
Select or cancel selection of the active card.	Ctrl+Spacebar

Extend the selection to the previous card and cancel selection of cards after the starting point.	Shift+Up Arrow
Extend the selection to the next card and cancel selection of cards before the starting point.	Shift+Down Arrow
Extend the selection to the previous card, regardless of the starting point.	Ctrl+Shift+Up Arrow
Extend the selection to the next card, regardless of the starting point.	Ctrl+Shift+Down Arrow
Extend the selection to the first card in the list.	Shift+Home
Extend the selection to the last card in the list.	Shift+End
Extend the selection to the first card on the previous page.	Shift+Page Up
Extend the selection to the last card on the last page.	Shift+Page Down

Move between fields in an open card

To use the following keys, make sure a field in a card is selected. To select a field when a card is selected, click the field.

Action	Shortcut
Move to the next field and control.	Tab
Move to the previous field and control.	Shift+Tab
Close the active card.	Enter

Move between characters in a field.

To use the following keys, make sure a field in a card is selected. To select a field when a card is selected, click the field.

Action	Shortcut
Add a line in a multiline field.	Enter
Move to the beginning of a line.	Home
Move to the end of a line.	End
Move to the beginning of a multiline field.	Page Up
Move to the end of a multiline field.	Page Down
Move to the previous line in a multiline field.	Up Arrow
Move to the next line in a multiline field.	Down Arrow
Move to the previous character in a field.	Left Arrow
Move to the next character in a field.	Right Arrow

Timeline view (Tasks)

When an item is selected

Action	Shortcut
Select the previous item.	Left Arrow
Select the next item.	Right Arrow
Select several adjacent items.	Shift+Left Arrow or Shift+Right Arrow

Select several nonadjacent items.	Ctrl+Left Arrow+Spacebar or Ctrl+Right Arrow+Spacebar
Open the selected items.	Enter
Select the first item on the timeline (if items are not grouped) or the first item in the group.	Home
Select the last item on the timeline (if items are not grouped) or the last item in the group.	End
Display (without selecting) the first item on the timeline (if items are not grouped) or the first item in the group.	Ctrl+Home
Display (without selecting) the last item on the timeline (if items are not grouped) or the last item in the group.	Ctrl+End

When a group is selected

Action	**Shortcut**
Expand the group.	Enter or Right Arrow
Collapse the group.	Enter or Left Arrow
Select the previous group.	Up Arrow
Select the next group.	Down Arrow
Select the first group on the timeline.	Home
Select the last group on the timeline.	End
Select the first item on screen in an expanded group or the first item off screen to the right.	Right Arrow

When a unit of time on the time scale for days is selected.

Action	Shortcut
Move back in increments of time that are the same as those shown on the time scale.	Left Arrow
Move forward in increments of time that are the same as those shown on the time scale.	Right Arrow
Switch between active view, To-Do Bar, Search and back to active view.	Tab and Shift+Tab

Calendar Day/Week/Month view

Action	Shortcut
View from 1 through 9 days.	Alt+key for number of days
View 10 days.	Alt+0 (zero)
Switch to weeks.	Alt+Minus Sign
Switch to months.	Alt+=
Move between **Calendar**, **TaskPad**, and the **Folder List**.	Ctrl+Tab or F6
Select the previous appointment.	Shift+Tab
Go to the previous day.	Left Arrow
Go to the next day.	Right Arrow
Go to the same day in the next week.	Alt+Down Arrow
Go to the same day in the previous week.	Alt+Up Arrow

Day view

Action	Shortcut
Select the time that begins your work day.	HOME

Select the time that ends your work day.	END
Select the previous block of time.	Up Arrow
Select the next block of time.	Down Arrow
Select the block of time at the top of the screen.	Page Up
Select the block of time at the bottom of the screen.	Page Down
Extend or reduce the selected time.	Shift+Up Arrow or Shift+Down Arrow, respectively
Move an appointment up or down.	With the cursor in the appointment, Alt+Up Arrow or Alt+Down Arrow, respectively
Change an appointment's start or end time.	With the cursor in the appointment, Alt+Shift+Up Arrow or Alt+Shift+Down Arrow, respectively
Move selected item to the same day in the next week.	Alt+Down Arrow
Move selected item to the same day in the previous week.	Alt+Up Arrow

Week view

Action	Shortcut
Go to the start of work hours for the selected day.	Home
Go to the end of work hours for the selected day.	End
Go up one page view in the selected day.	Page Up
Go down one page view in the selected day.	Page Down
Change the duration of the selected block of time.	Shift+Left Arrow, Shift+Right Arrow, Shift+Up Arrow, or Shift+Down Arrow; or Shift+Home or Shift+End

Month view

Action	Shortcut
Go to the first day of the week.	Home
Go to the same day of the week in the previous page.	Page Up
Go to the same day of the week in the next page.	Page Down

Date Navigator

Action	Shortcut
Go to the first day of the current week.	Alt+Home

Go to the last day of the current week.	Alt+End
Go to the same day in the previous week.	Alt+Up Arrow
Go to the same day in the next week.	Alt+Down Arrow

End of Topic.

A fresh topic

Outlook 2016 Keyboard Shortcuts for Macintosh.

Frequently Used Shortcuts.

Action	Shortcut
Save an item	⌘+ S
Print an item	⌘+ P
Undo the last action	⌘+ Z
Redo the last action	⌘+ Y
Minimize the active window	⌘+ M
Create a new folder in the navigation pane	Shift + ⌘+ N
Create new email (in Mail view)	⌘+ N
Hide the reading pane or show it on the right	⌘+ Backslash (\ )

Hide the reading pane or show it below	Shift + ⌘+ Backslash (\ )
Move the selected item to a different folder	Shift + ⌘+ M
Copy the selected item to a different folder	Shift + ⌘+ C
Select all items in the item list, if the item list is the active pane	⌘+ A
Minimize or expand the ribbon	Options + ⌘+ R
Hide Outlook	⌘+ H
Quit Outlook	⌘+ Q
Start dictation	Fn + Fn
Insert emoji	Control + ⌘+ Space

Work in Windows and Dialogs.

Action	Shortcut
Go to Mail view	⌘+ 1
Go to Calendar view	⌘+ 2
Go to Contacts view	⌘+ 3
Go to Tasks view	⌘+ 4
Go to Notes view	⌘+ 5
Open the Sync Status window or make it the active window	⌘+ 7
Open the Sync Errors or make it the active window	⌘+ 8
Open the Contacts Search window	⌘+ O
Open the Outlook Preferences dialog box	⌘+ Comma (,)

Cycle forward through open windows	⌘+ Tilde (~)
Cycle back through open windows	Shift + ⌘+ Tilde (~)
Close the active window	⌘+ W
Open the selected item	⌘+ O
Move forward through controls in a window	Tab
Move back through controls in a window	Shift + Tab

Use Search.

Action	Shortcut
Search current folder	Option + ⌘+ F
Do an advanced search in Outlook (add Item Contains filter for searching)	Shift + ⌘+ F
Find text within an item	⌘+ F
Find the next instance of the text you searched for in an item	⌘+ G
Find the previous instance of the text you searched for in an item	⌘+ Shift + G

Send and Receive Mail.

Action	Shortcut
Create a new message	⌘+ N
Send the open message	⌘+ Return
Send all messages in the Outbox and receive all incoming messages	⌘+ K

Send all the messages in the Outbox	Shift + ⌘+ K
Save the open message and store it in the Drafts folder	⌘+ S
Add an attachment to the open message	⌘+ E
Open the Spelling and Grammar dialog box	⌘+ Colon (:)
Check recipient names in the open messages	Control + ⌘+ C
Reply to the sender of the message or, if the message is from a mailing list, reply to the mailing list	⌘+ R
Reply to all	Shift+ ⌘+ R
Forward the message	⌘+ J
Open the selected message in a separate window	⌘+ O
Clear the flag for the selected message	Option + ⌘+ Apostrophe (')
Mark the selected message as junk mail	⌘+ Shift + J
Mark the selected message as not junk mail	⌘+ Shift + Option + J
Display the previous message	Control + Opening bracket ([ )
Display the next message	Control + Closing bracket ( ])
Navigate to the previous pane in the Mail view	Shift + Control + Opening bracket ([ )
Navigate to the next pane in the Mail view	Shift + Control + Closing bracket ( ])

Move the selected message to a folder	Shift + ⌘+ M
Decrease the display size of text in an open message or in the reading pane	⌘+ Hyphen (-)
Increase the display size of text in an open message or in the reading pane	⌘+ Plus sign (+)
Scroll down to the next screen of text or, if you are at the end of a message, display the next message	Spacebar
Scroll up to the previous screen of text or, if you are at the beginning of a message, display the previous message	Shift+ Spacebar
Delete the selected message	Delete
Permanently delete the selected message	Shift + Delete
Delete the current message, and, if the message window is open, close it	⌘+ Delete
Mark selected messages as read	⌘+ T
Mark selected messages as unread	Shift + ⌘+ T
Mark all messages in a folder as read	Option + ⌘+ T

Use The Calendar.

Action	Shortcut
Open the Calendar window	⌘+ 2
Create a new appointment	⌘+ N
Open the selected calendar event	⌘+ O
Delete the calendar event	Delete
Switch the view to include today	⌘+ T

In Day view, move to the previous day. In Week and Work Week views, move to the previous week. In Month view, move to the previous month.	⌘+ Left arrow
In Day view, move to the next day. In Week and Work Week views, move to the next week. In Month view, move to the next month.	⌘+ Right arrow
Navigate to the previous pane in the Calendar view	Shift + Control + Opening bracket ([ )
Navigate to the next pane in the Calendar view	Shift + Control + Closing bracket ( ])

Work With People and Contacts.

Action	Shortcut
Create a new contact	⌘+ N
Open the selected contact	⌘+ O
Delete the contact	Delete
Close the current open contact and open the previous contact	Control + Opening bracket ([ )
Close the current open contact and open the next contact	Control + Closing bracket ( ])
Navigate to the previous pane in the People view	Shift+ Control + Opening bracket ([ )
Navigate to the next pane in the People view	Shift + Control + Closing bracket ( ])

Manage Tasks.

Action	Shortcut
Move to the Task window	⌘+ 4
Create a new task	⌘+ N
Open the selected task	⌘+ O
Delete the task	Delete
Close the current open task and open the previous task in the Tasks list	Control + Opening bracket ([ )
Close the current open task and open the next task in the Tasks list	Control + Closing bracket ( ])
Navigate to the previous pane in the Tasks view	Shift + Control + Opening bracket ([ )
Navigate to the next pane in the Tasks view	Shift + Control + Closing bracket ( ])

Use Notes.

Action	Shortcut
Move to the Notes window	⌘+ 5
Create a new note	⌘+ N
Open the selected note	⌘+ O
Delete the note	Delete
Close the current open note and open the previous note in the Notes list	Control + Opening bracket ([ )
Close the current open note and open the next note in the Notes list	Control + Closing bracket ( ])

Navigate to the previous pane in the Notes view	Shift + Control + Opening bracket ([ )
Navigate to the next pane in the Notes view	Shift + Control + Closing bracket ( ])
Send a note as an email	⌘+ J
Send a note as an HTML attachment to an email	Control + ⌘+ J First place the focus on the note in the list of notes.

Edit and Format Text.

Action	Shortcut
Cut the selected text to the clipboard	⌘+ X
Copy a selection to the clipboard	⌘+ C
Paste a selection from the clipboard	⌘+ V
Paste a selection from the clipboard and match the destination style	Shift + Option + ⌘+ V
Make the selected text bold	⌘+ B
Make the selected text italic	⌘+ I
Underline the selected text	⌘+ U
Strike through the selected text	Shift + ⌘+ X
Insert a hyperlink	Control + ⌘+ K
Move the cursor left one character	Left arrow

Move the cursor right one character	Right arrow
Move the cursor up one line	Up arrow
Move the cursor down one line	Down arrow
Move the cursor to the beginning of the current paragraph	Option + Up arrow
Move the cursor to the end of the current paragraph	Option + Down arrow
Move the cursor to the beginning of the current word	Option + Left arrow
Move the cursor to the end of the current word	Option + Right arrow
Decrease indent	⌦+ Opening brace ({)
Increase indent	⌦+ Closing brace ({)
Delete the character to the left of the cursor, or delete the selected text	Delete
Delete the character to the right side of the cursor, or delete the selected text	⌦ If your keyboard doesn't have a ⌦key, use FN + Delete.
Insert a tab stop	Tab
Move the cursor to the beginning of the line	⌘+ Left arrow
Move the cursor to the end of the line	⌘+ Right arrow
Move the cursor to the top of the message body	⌘+ Up arrow
Move the cursor to the bottom of the message body	⌘+ Down arrow

Move the cursor to the beginning of the selected text	⌘+ Home
Move the cursor to the end of the selected text	⌘+ End
Scroll up	Page up
Scroll down	Page down

Flag Messages, Contacts, and Tasks For Follow up.

Action	Shortcut
Flag the selected item for follow up, with Today as Due Date	Control + 1
Flag the selected item for follow up, with Tomorrow as Due Date	Control + 2
Flag the selected item for follow up, with This Week as Due Date	Control + 3
Flag the selected item for follow up, with Next Week as Due Date	Control + 4
Flag the selected item for follow up, with No Due Date	Control + 5
Flag the selected item for follow up, and add a custom Due Date	Control + 6
Flag the selected item for follow up, and add a reminder	Control + Equal sign (=)
Mark the selected item as Complete	Control + Zero (0)
Clear the selected item's follow-up flag	Option + ⌘+ Apostrophe (')

CHAPTER 8.

Tips, Tricks, Techniques, and Keyboard Shortcuts for use in GMX Mail.

Introduction: This is a free email service that supports advertisement provided by GMX (Global Mail eXchange or Global Message eXchange) established in 1997.

A fresh topic

Your Unlimited Email Storage in GMX.

Imagine how easy it would be to store and access all your emails in one place. With GMX, it is just that simple! Unlimited email storage protects your old and new emails from accidental deletion. Keep all your emails in one place with GMX email storage.

Unlimited email storage is all you need

There are so many reasons to use unlimited email storage! You may think that having so many emails in one place can get really messy, but GMX has implemented a solution for this. You can easily filter emails by date, subject, sender or even content! You will be able to find your emails fast and

134

easily whenever you need them. GMX email storage offers a lot more than this: your emails can be stored forever at GMX, while other providers offer to save your emails for a limited time and with limited mailbox storage. Are you looking for that email that your friend sent you years ago with an awesome cake recipe? GMX has it stored just for you!

Email management with unlimited inbox storage.

You can keep all your emails within GMX unlimited email storage. Advanced email security keeps them all safe. Take advantage of the unlimited possibilities at GMX!

Learn how to create email account with GMX here.

Mobile email – Your emails anywhere you are.

You are no longer forced to use only one computer. Nowadays, with a wide range of mobile devices, you can always be on the move and still receive and send emails. Isn't it awesome? No matter where you are! At home, in the office, on the other side of the world - mobile email access allows you to send and receive emails! Whether you have a notebook, a tablet or any Android smartphone or iPhone, GMX mobile email will be there for you to check your inbox!

Nothing better than email on the go.

Having a smartphone is a big relief – this tiny mobile device is your window to the world, always at your fingertips. With GMX mobile email access, you can send an email while spending a lazy day on the beach in Miami to your friend while she climbs Mount McKinley, or organize your week in your online calendar. Wherever you are, mobile email makes this possible – fast and secure!

Stay in touch with mobile email access!

You will never miss an important email or date anymore! Thanks to mobile email, you can check your emails or your online calendar wherever you are. Having a mobile device and mobile email allows you to be connected to the world for as long, or as short, as you want!

Mail Collector: the best email software for organizing your email accounts.

We all know how important managing your email is: if it doesn't work the way it should, your emails will be a mess and you will be stuck for hours trying to find the one you are looking for! In order to make emailing easier, GMX has created an email software to organize all email accounts in the best possible way. You will simply love managing multiple accounts in one place – this is what Mail Collector from GMX is all about.

Email wherever you are.

If you have multiple email accounts, it is important to manage them well and to have universal access to all of them. With GMX email software, all those issues are solved. Wherever you are you have the great possibility to access and manage all your emails from different accounts in one place thanks to GMX mail forwarding feature. Just sign up for your free GMX email account and forward to it emails from other accounts.

Mail Collector: do well with multiple email accounts.

You may use a lot of different email providers, but that won't be a problem anymore! GMX email software will keep them all safe in one GMX email account. This feature allows you to keep all of your accounts in one place – your private as well as your business email accounts.

Easy-to-use email - With everything you ever needed!

It's important to have an easy-to-use email. And why? It makes everything easier and faster, you can enjoy more free time! GMX strives for their email usability to fulfill your needs. It's easy to handle email at GMX, and using it is even easier!

Discover GMX email!

To make emailing faster, GMX has developed a drag & drop function. What does this entail? It gets much easier to add attachments or to organize appointments in your online calendar. It's very easy to use! Email with GMX also offers other great features. There is place at GMX for all your emails. Send and receive emails anywhere you are with GMX Mail mobile service. Keep all your email accounts in one place thanks to Mail Collector - and much more. These are just some examples of GMX's high email usability.

Your user-friendly email.

Email usability is what GMX team has in mind when they create GMX email accounts. They know how busy your days can be and that every second counts. This easy-to-use email has been designed taking your precious time into consideration. They provide email services you can access wherever you are.

End of Topic.

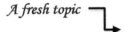

Most Commonly Used Keyboard Shortcuts in GMX.

Use the following list of keyboard shortcuts to enhance your productivity in GMX.

Shortcuts for Open New Message:

Action	Shortcut
Open a message	Ctrl+O

Create new message (when in Mail)	Ctrl+N
Create new message	Ctrl+Shift+M

Navigation Shortcut Keys:

Action	Shortcut
Switch to inbox	Ctrl+Shift+I
Switch to outbox	Ctrl+Shift+O
Open address book	Ctrl+Shift+B
Open a folder list	Ctrl+Y
Read next message (with a message open)	Ctrl+. (period)
Read previous message (with a message open)	Ctrl+, (comma)
Read previous message (with a message open)	F6

Shortcut Keys for Changing Messages:

Action	Shortcut
Delete open item	Ctrl+D
Mark as read	Ctrl+Q
Mark as unread	Ctrl+U
Find or replace (with a message open)	F4
Find next (with a message open)	Shift+F4
Print	Ctrl+P
Mark for download	Ctrl+Alt+M

Clear Mark for Download	Ctrl+Alt+U
Mark as not junk mail	Ctrl+Alt+J
Toggle follow-up flag	Insert

Tools:

Action	Shortcut
Check for new mail	F9
Display send/receive progress	Ctrl+B
Send mail	Alt+S
Reply to selected message	Ctrl+R
Reply all	Ctrl+Shift+R
Forward selected mail	Ctrl+F
Forward as attachment	Ctrl+Alt+F

CHAPTER 9.

Tips, Tricks, Techniques, and Keyboard Shortcuts for AOL Mail.

Introduction: AOL (America Online) is a free web-based email service provided by AOL incorporated.

A fresh topic

What are the Minimum System Requirements for AOL Mail?

Learn what the minimum system requirements and browser versions are to get the best AOL Mail experience.

To get the best AOL Mail experience, we (AOL team) recommend you download the latest version of your web browser. Below are the operating systems and web browser versions that work best for the Standard Version of AOL Mail and those that work with the Basic Version of AOL Mail.

Click the links below to download the latest browser version:

- Download the latest version of Internet Explorer

- Download the latest version of Firefox
- Download the latest version of Safari

Operating systems that work best with Standard Version of AOL Mail

Windows 7 and 8 / Windows XP (Professional and Home)

- Latest version of Internet Explorer
- Latest version of Firefox
- Latest version of Chrome
- Latest version of Safari
- AOL Desktop Software 9.0 and above

Mac OS X 10.5 and above

- Latest version of Firefox
- Latest version of Safari
- Latest version of Chrome

Operating systems that work with Basic Version of AOL Mail

Windows 7 and 8 / Windows XP (Professional and Home)

- Internet Explorer 8.0 and above
- Firefox 3.0 and above
- Chrome
- Safari 4.0 and above

Windows 2000

- Internet Explorer 8.0 and above
- Firefox 3.0 and above

Windows 98

- Internet Explorer 8.0 and above

Mac OS X

- Safari 1.3 and above
- Firefox 2.0 and above

Operating systems that work with mobile web version of AOL Mail

- iOS 5 and above
- Android 4.1 and above
- Blackberry 10
- Nexus 7
- WebOS Products

End of Topic.

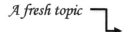

A fresh topic

AOL Mail: Features and Actions.

Learn about some of the top features of your AOL Mail account, like sending text messages and using AIM in your inbox, managing your AOL Calendar, creating and using folders, and searching your mail.

Sending Text Messages and Using AIM in AOL Mail.

How do I send a text message from my AOL Mail inbox?

Here's how to send texts to friends and family members' mobile devices from AOL Mail.

First, here are the mobile service providers that AOL Mail currently supports:

Verizon	AT&T
Sprint	Google Voice
T-Mobile	Boost (1-way messaging only)
Virgin Mobile	US Cellular
Alltel	Cricket Wireless
nTelos Wireless	Centennial Cellular
Immix Wireless	Cellular One
Appalachian Wireless	Bluegrass Cellular
COM TMI Wireless	GCI/Alaska DigiTel
Illinois Valley	Inland Cellular
Nex-Tech	United Wireless
West Central	Metro PCS*

*Metro PCS: Messaging is only supported on select Metro PCS plans. If you use Metro PCS and you run into issues sending or receiving messages via AOL, please contact Metro PCS for more information.

Also, texting is currently <u>only</u> available to U.S. mobile numbers (no international numbers and no landlines).

OK, here goes:

1. In the lower-left panel of your Inbox, click the **AIM** button (the 'a' icon).

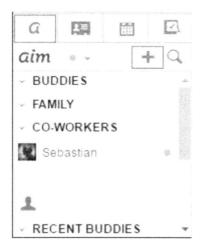

2. Click the + (plus) sign.

3. In the "New IM" window that opens, click the **New IM** button and select **Switch to SMS**.

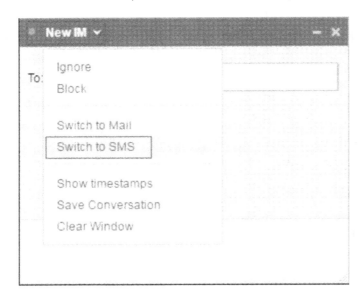

4. In the "New Text" Window, enter the mobile number (including area code) that you'd like to text. Type all 10 digits together -- no spaces, hyphens, parentheses or any other marks are necessary.

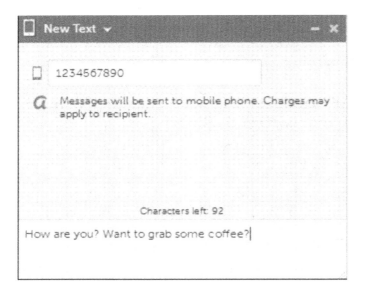

5. Type your text in the message field and hit **enter** on your keyboard.

That's it! You'll get replies to your text messages in the lower right corner of your AOL Mail window.

Note: Sending and receiving text messages in AOL Mail is free, but charges may apply for the person you're texting -- depending on his/her plan.

How do I access my AIM Buddy List in AOL Mail?

Wondering if your AIM buddies are online? Check your buddy list in AOL Mail.

To access your AIM buddy list in AOL Mail:

1. In the lower-left panel of your Inbox, click the 'A' - that's the new AIM logo!

2. To start a chat with a buddy, click their Username in the AIM window.

3. In the bottom right of your inbox, in the IM window, type your message and then hit enter on your keyboard.

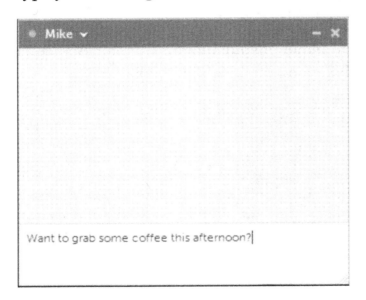

Tada! Now, who are you going to chat with?

How do I set up Facebook Chat in AOL Mail?

Facebook no longer supports chat integration for third party clients such as AOL Mail. For more information, please read <u>Facebook ends support for AIM chat integration</u>

How do I block someone using AIM in AOL Mail?

Are you receiving unwanted instant messages? You can block unwanted IMs in AOL Mail and stop a specific Username from sending you IMs in the future.

To block someone from sending you IMs:

1. In your AIM window, find the person you'd like to block and click the *i* to the right of their name.

2. Under their Username, click **Block**.

That's it! A small red circle with a **minus** will appear by the Username that you blocked.

How do I save IM conversations in AOL Mail?

Ever forget something important that was sent to you as an instant message? Me too. Well now you can save an IM conversation for future reference in AOL Mail.

To save an IM conversation in AOL Mail:

1. At the top of the IM window, next to the person's name, click the **down arrow** drop-down menu and then click **Save Conversation**.

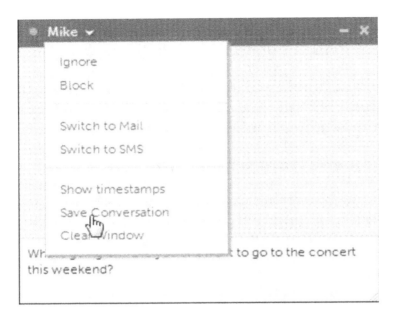

2. That's it! In the left panel, under My Folders, click the **Saved Chats** folder to see all your saved IM conversations.

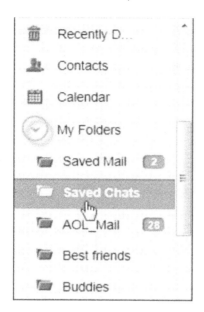

Managing Your Calendar in AOL Mail

How do I subscribe to a calendar in AOL Mail?

If you want to view a calendar that is not on your list of calendars, you have to subscribe to it.

To subscribe to a calendar:

1. In the left panel, click **Calendar**.

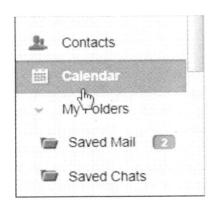

2. Above your Calendar, in the upper right, click the **More** drop-down menu and then click **Subscribe to a Calendar**.

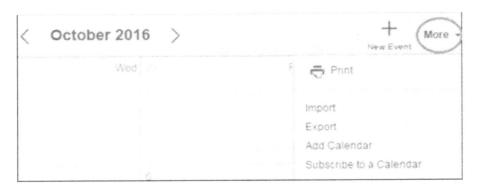

3. In the **Subscribe to a Calendar** box, enter the name of the Calendar you want to subscribe to and then enter the URL of the calendar in the bottom box.

Subscribe to a Calendar   Or Add a Personal Calendar

Enter Calendar Name

Enter the ical URL for calendar you want to subscribe to The calendar will update automatically

Calendar URL

Cancel

Note: The URL can be for any public calendar in iCalendar format.

4. Click **Subscribe**.

How do I change the time zone and hourly display on my calendar?

You can adjust the time zone and display on your AOL Calendar under settings.

Here's how to:

Set Time Zone

Adjust time display

Can I print my AOL Calendar?

Yep. Here's how:

To print your AOL Calendar:

1. Above your AOL Calendar, in the upper right, click the **More** drop-down menu, and then click **Print**.

2. You'll see a message that says: "To print, select Print from this window's File menu". Click **OK**.

Note: If you're using a Mac, you'll find the print option on your web browser under File at the very top. If you're using a Windows PC, you'll find your web browsers Print option located in the upper right of your browser window (IE, Chrome) or in the upper left (FireFox).

How do I create or add a calendar?

Using the Calendar feature in AOL Mail is a great way to keep track of your important events and dates. You can create and view multiple calendars --- one for your family, one for your bridge club, and another for your soccer team. You can view multiple calendars either one at a time or in combination, enabling you to coordinate schedules and stay on top of your friends' and family's plans.

Note: If you want to view a calendar that doesn't appear on your list of calendars, you need to subscribe to that calendar.

To create or add a calendar:

1. There are two ways to easily add a Calendar event.

The first way: In the lower-left panel, you can click the **Events** tab (the second from the right) and then click the + sign.

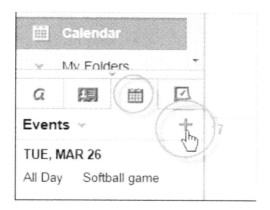

The second way: In the left panel, click **Calendar** to open your AOL Calendar and then in the upper right click **New Event**.

2. In the 'Add Event' window that appears, type the name of the event. You can also:

- Adjust the date of the event
- Make it a repeating event
- Set a reminder

- Add a location
- Add notes about the event

3. When you're finished, at the bottom, click **Add Event**.

How do I import events from other calendar programs?

Did you know you can import calendar events from programs such as Microsoft Outlook in to your AOL Mail Calendar?

Here's how:

1. Sign in to your AOL Calendar.

2. In the upper right, click the **More** button and then click **Import** from the drop-menu.

3. Next to **Calendar File**, click the **Browse** button.

4. Locate the file that you wish to import, select it, and then click the **Open** button.

5. Click the drop-down arrow next to **Target Calendar** and choose which calendar you want to import the events into.

6. Next to **File Type**, choose the option that matches the file you'd like to import and then click **Import**.

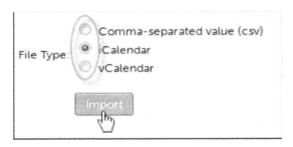

All done! The events included in the file will now be displayed on your selected AOL Mail Calendar.

How do I search for events in my AOL Calendar?

The Calendar in AOL Mail has built in search features to help you find Events easily and quickly.

To Search for Events in your Calendar:

Note: The search feature searches for Events on your Calendar that are two months behind to six months ahead of today's date.

1. If you are using AOL Mail, in the left panel, click **Calendar** or load your Calendar at calendar.aol.com.

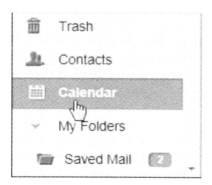

2. In the upper left, in the **Search Calendar** box, type the name of the event that you're searching for, and then click the **magnifying glass** icon or hit **Enter** on your keyboard.

Search example using AOL Mail:

Search example in your AOL Calendar:

3. In the main reading pane, you'll see a list of search results matching what you entered in the "Search Calendar" box. Click the Event to see more details. Happy hunting!

How do I add a To-Do in AOL Mail?

Ever have trouble remembering people's birthdays or upcoming events? Your **To Do** list in AOL Mail helps you never forget another important date or event.

To schedule a To Do in AOL Mail:

1. In the left panel, click **To Do's**.

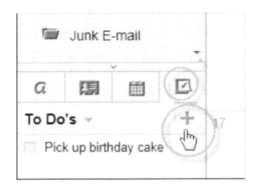

2. In the 'Add a To Do' box that appears, type the name of your To Do and then hit enter/return on your keyboard.

Note: To add more information like a Date, a Reminder, or Notes about your To Do, click the name of the event.

That's it! Your To Do will be added to your To Do's list, and if you added a date, it'll be added to your AOL Calendar.

How do I add holidays to my AOL Calendar?

While new Calendar accounts don't come pre-loaded with holidays, it's easy to subscribe to a public calendar that will add them to your AOL Calendar.

You can choose a US-holiday calendar, a calendar showing Canadian holidays, or get holiday calendars from other countries and cultural traditions. There are also calendars showing dates of historical interest, lunar calendars, even game schedules of sports teams.

Any calendar just needs to be in iCal format. Directories of these (such as http://www.icalshare.com) are easily available.

Here's how to add holidays (or any other calendar) to your AOL Calendar:

1. Sign into your account at mail.aol.com.

2. On the left side of your inbox, click **Calendar**.

3. In the upper-right corner of your Calendar, click **More** and select **Subscribe to a calendar**.

4. Under "Subscribe to a Calendar", type a name for this calendar -- such as Holidays.

5. In the box under "Enter the ical URL for calendar", type (or copy & paste) the URL for the calendar. Make sure the URL begins with http://.

For example: http://ical.mac.com/ical/US32Holidays.ics

(That's a public US Holiday calendar.)

6. Click **Subscribe**.

Done!

How can I easily edit events on my AOL Calendar?

You can drag and drop events in your AOL Calendar to different days, months, and time slots as desired. This is an easy way to shift your events around when you need to make quick updates to your calendar.

You can drag an event to a different day to quickly change the date of an event, or you can drag an event to a different time slot in the same day.

Notes:

- If you are dragging a repeating event, the additional occurrences of the event will not change.
- In the **Day** view of your calendar, you can only drag events to a different time slot.

To drag an event from one day to another
1. On the upper right of the AOL Calendar, click the **Month**, **Week**, or **Day** button.

2. Click and hold the event that you wish to move, and then drag and drop it on the date or time slot that you want to move the event to.

You can now easily make changes to your AOL Calendar at any time!

Creating and Using Folders.

How do I create a new folder in AOL Mail?

Creating a new folder in AOL Mail is a snap.

Here's how:

1. In the left panel, next to My Folders, click the + icon.

2. Below your list of folders, in the text box provided, enter the name of your new folder and then click the + icon or hit enter on your keyboard.

Tada! You'll see your new folder listed alphabetically with the others under My Folders (Saved Mail is always listed first).

How do I rename a folder?

To rename a folder that you've created in AOL Mail:

1. In the left panel, under "My Folders" click the **gear** icon to the right of the folder that you'd like to rename.

2. In the Edit Folder window, change the name of the folder in the box and then click **Save.**

How do I delete a folder?

Having second thoughts about the folder you created? Deleting it is a snap.

Here's how:

1. In the left panel, under "My Folders", click the **gear** icon to the right of the folder that you'd like to delete.

2. In the Edit Folder window, click the **Delete** link.

3. In the confirmation window, click **OK**.

Presto! Your folder is gone.

What is the Drafts folder in AOL Mail?

Ever sit down to write an email, but right in the middle, need to step out and run some errands? The Drafts folder stores messages that you haven't finished writing, letting you complete and send your email at a later time.

To save a message to your Drafts folder:

1. Above your email, next to Send, click the **Save** button.

2. To access the message that you just saved, in the left panel, click the **Drafts folder**.

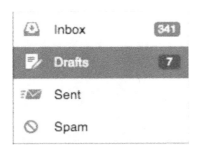

Tada! Your message is waiting for you in the Drafts folder. Feel free to run some errands and return to your email whenever you'd like!

Saving Emails and Moving Messages.

How do I move emails into a folder or back into my Inbox?

Moving emails into folders in AOL Mail is a great way to organize your mail. Because the messages are stored online under **My Folders**, you can access them from any computer when you sign in to your account.

Here's how to:

Move a single message into a folder

To move a single message into a folder: The easiest way to move a single message is to left-click and hold the email that you'd like to move, and then drag-and-drop it into the folder you'd like to move it into (let go of the left-click button on your mouse above the folder).

Move multiple messages into a folder

To move multiple messages into a folder:

1. Click the boxes next to the emails you'd like to move.

2. Above your list of messages, click the **More** drop-down menu, and then click the folder you'd like to move the emails to.

Note: If you want to create a new folder, click the **More** drop-down menu and then click **New Folder** (it's at the bottom). Type the name of your new folder in the box provided and then click the + icon to add the folder to your list.

Voila! Your messages have been moved. You can access your saved messages by clicking **My Folders** in the left panel.

Can I save emails in AOL Mail?

Yes!

Here's how:

1. Click the box next to the email(s) you'd like to save.

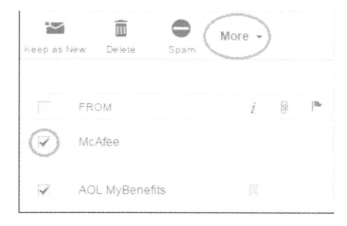

2. Above your list of messages, click the **More** drop-down menu, and then under "Move To", click **Saved Mail**.

Voila! Your message has been moved to your Saved Mail folder.

Searching Your Mail and Using Email Filters.

How do I search for an email in AOL Mail?

Trouble finding a certain email? The search feature in AOL Mail is a great way to quickly and easily find a particular message.

To search for an email in AOL Mail:

1. In the **Search Mail** box, located to the left above your mail folders, type a name, email address, or keyword that is included in the email that you're looking for, and then click the **magnifying glass** icon (or hit **Enter** on your keyboard.)

2. In the main reading pane, a list of search results will appear. If you see the email you're looking for, click it to open it.

3. Or, to filter the search results even more, near the upper-right corner, click the **Refine** drop-down menu to separate the results **By Folder**, **By Sender**, or **By Message Type**. Happy hunting!

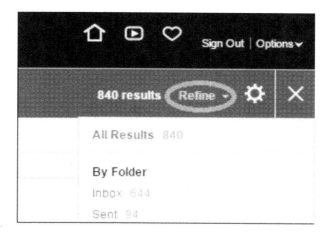

Problems?

If you're having issues with the Search function in AOL Mail, AOL team wants to know about it!

Please click the **Need help? Email us** button below, and write them the details of what you're experiencing. They'd like to know how you are searching (by sender? subject? words in a message? parts of words?), and what kind of results you are getting vs. what you're expecting to see. They appreciate your feedback.

How do I search for Contacts in AOL Mail?

Looking for a particular contact? Try using the search field in AOL Mail to find the person or email address that you're looking for quickly and easily.

To search for a Contact:

1. In the left panel, click **Contacts**.

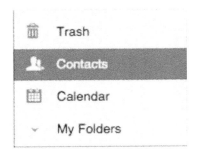

2. Above your inbox, in the **Search Contacts** box, enter the contact name or email address you want to search for.

That's it! You'll see a list of contacts matching the person or email address you entered in the search field. Sweet!

How do I search for events in my AOL Calendar?

The Calendar in AOL Mail has built in search features to help you find Events easily and quickly.

To Search for Events in your Calendar:

Note: The search feature searches for Events on your Calendar that are two months behind to six months ahead of today's date.

1. If you are using AOL Mail, in the left panel, click **Calendar** or load your Calendar at calendar.aol.com.

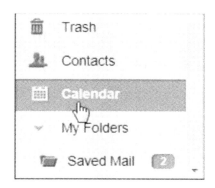

2. In the upper left, in the **Search Calendar** box, type the name of the event that you're searching for, and then click the **magnifying glass** icon or hit **Enter** on your keyboard.

Search example using AOL Mail:

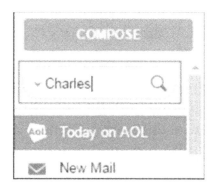

Search example in your AOL Calendar:

3. In the main reading pane, you'll see a list of search results matching what you entered in the "Search Calendar" box. Click the Event to see more details. Happy hunting!

How do I sort emails in AOL Mail?

Your emails in AOL Mail are automatically sorted by date, but did you know you can also sort your messages by sender, subject, read or unread messages, and emails that you've flagged?

To sort your emails:

1. In the left panel, click the folder that contains the emails you'd like to sort.

2. Click one of the column headings at the top of the email list to sort by one of the following options:

Note: The column header will turn a slightly darker shade of gray when selected and will display an up arrow to indicate the list is being sorted in ascending order or a down arrow to indicate the list is sorted in descending order.

- Click the **From** column heading to sort messages alphabetically by the sender's email address.
- Click the **paper clip** icon to sort messages by emails with attachments.
- Click the **Subject** column to sort messages alphabetically by the text on the subject line.
- Click the **Date** column to sort messages by when they were received or sent.

- Click the **Flag** icon to sort messages by emails that are flagged.

That's it! Pretty cool, right?

How do I set up filters in AOL Mail?

You can "filter" incoming mail in AOL Mail to make certain emails go directly into the folders where you want them -- or, to make unwanted mail from specific senders go straight into Trash.

You can also use Filters to set up Alerts to notify you in AIM or on your mobile phone when certain email arrives. (Alert me anytime I get a message containing the words "You absolutely rock", for example.)

Note: You can create up to 50 filters.

Here's how to set up Filters and Alerts: 1. In the upper-right corner, next to your Username, click the **down arrow**, and then click **Mail Settings**.

2. In the left panel, click **Filters and Alerts**, and then click the **Create filter** button in the middle of the page. Check it out:

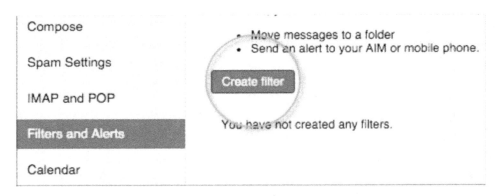

3. The "Create Filter" window opens. Give your Filter (or Alert) a name, and fill in as much detail as you'd like:

4. Under "Look for incoming messages matching all of the following," define the criteria for the filter. That is, the emails that the filter will capture.

5. Under "Do the following with matched messages," click the **Move to folder...** drop-down arrow if you'd like to send these messages to a folder (you don't *have* to do this; messages can just keep coming into your inbox), then check (or leave blank) a box beside the type of Alert you'd like to send yourself when these messages arrive. (You don't *have* to select an Alert.)

6. OK, great. Done! Click **Create** to save your work.

How do I delete a filter in AOL Mail?

If you have a filter set up that is sending mail to a folder like your Spam folder, personal folder, or Trash, you can delete it to start sending the filtered messages back to your Inbox.

To delete a filter:

1. In the upper right, under your Username, click **Options** and then click **Mail Settings**.

2. In the left panel, click **Filters and Alerts**.

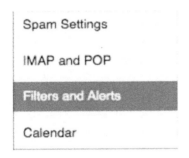

3. In the main window, you'll see a list of all of your filters. Move your pointer over the filter that you'd like to delete, and click the "**X**" next to Edit.

Priority	Filter Name		Criteria and Actions	
1	New Filter	Edit	Find:	From: johndoeusername
			Do:	Move to folder: Friends

That's it! Messages that were once filtered will now appear in your Inbox.

The Trash Folder and Deleting Mail.

How do I delete an email or multiple emails in AOL Mail?

Is your AOL Mail inbox getting a bit full? Deleting old emails will free up space and help organize your inbox. You can delete messages individually or clean out your entire inbox or folder with just a few clicks.

To delete an email:

1. Click the box to the left of the email that you'd like to delete. If you want to delete more than one email, click the box next to each message that you want to delete.

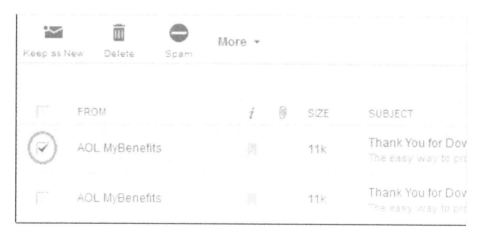

2. Above your mailbox, click the **Delete button** (the trash can icon).

To delete all the messages in a folder:

1. Above your list of messages, click the box just under the **Keep as New** button to select all of your emails.

2. Above your mailbox, click the **Delete button** (the trash can icon).

How do I recover an email that was recently deleted?

Accidentally delete an email? If it's been less than seven days since you deleted the message, you can still recover it.

To recover an email that has been deleted:

1. In the left panel, click **Trash**.

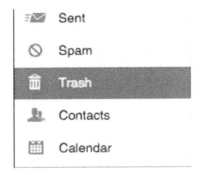

2. Click the box next to the email that you want to restore.

3. Above your list of messages, click the **More** drop-down menu, and then under 'Move to:', click where you'd like the message to be moved to.

Phew! That was close. Remember, you have up to 7 days to recover messages in your Trash. After that, emails will be permanently deleted so don't wait too long!

How long are emails stored in my AOL Mail Inbox?

Here's a quick look at how long messages are stored in your AOL Mail inbox.

Important:

Please remember that your emails will be permanently deleted and cannot be retrieved if your account is inactive. To keep your account active, you need to sign in to AOL Mail with your username and password at least once every 90 days.

Folder	Limits and Timelines
Inbox	Emails will remain in your **Inbox** folder until you delete them (even the emails that you've read).
Sent	Sent emails will remain in your **Sent** folder until you delete them.
Spam	Emails in your **Spam** folder will be automatically deleted after 5 days.
Recently Deleted or **Trash**	Emails you delete may be deleted immediately or may remain in your **Recently Deleted** or **Trash** folder for up to 7 days.
My Folders	Emails saved to any of the subfolders in your **My Folders** mail folder will never be deleted until you delete them.

AOL Desktop Software storage limits:

- If you're using the AOL Desktop Software, and have over 5,000 emails, you'll only see the most recent 5,000 messages. To see more than the most recent 5,000 emails, please open a web browser and sign in to your mail at mail.aol.com.
- The number of emails that can be saved to the Saved on My PC folder and its sub-folders is only limited by the space available on your hard disk.
- You can create up to 252 personal folders using the AOL Desktop Software.

How do I empty my Trash in AOL Mail?

To empty your Trash in AOL Mail:

1. In the left panel, click **Trash**.

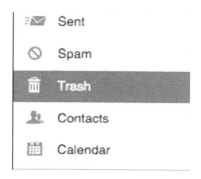

2. Click the check-box at the top of the left-most column in your inbox to select all the messages.

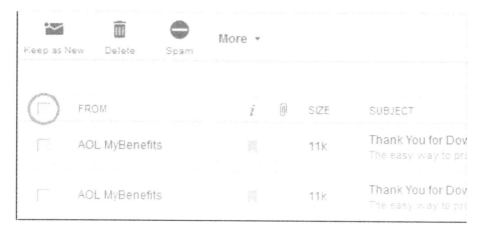

3. Above your list of messages, click the **Delete button**.

4. You'll see a box open with the message, "This action will permanently delete the selected messages. Click **OK** to proceed." Click **OK** -- and poof! They're gone.

Mailbox Tips.

How do I save my Username and Password on the AOL Mail sign in page?

Want quicker access to your AOL Mail? Save your Username and Password on the AOL Mail sign in page so you don't have to enter it each time you want to access your mail.

To save your Username and Password on the AOL Mail sign in page:

1. Go to mail.aol.com.

2. On the sign in page, enter your "Username or Email" and "Password" in the boxes provided, and then check the box next to "Remember Me".

3. Click **Sign In**.

Note: We recommend that you only use this feature on a computer or computers that are used or owned by you. Using this feature on a public computer, such as an internet kiosk at an airport, can place your mail security at risk and allow unwanted users access to your account.

You're Done! Now you can access your AOL Mail with just a click of your mouse. Sweet!

How do I resize the panels in my AOL Mail Inbox?

Need room to stretch out? You can resize the panels in AOL Mail to your liking.

The left panel lists your email folders, contacts, AIM Buddy List, calendar, and To-Dos, while the central panel is the main viewing area for your mail.

To resize a panel:

1. Move your pointer over the line between the main viewing area and the left panel and leave it there until your pointer turns into a double-sided arrow.

2. Click and hold your left mouse button and slide the bar in the desired direction.

Note: The left panel can't be completely removed from your computer screen. It can only be minimized. You can also adjust the size of the **From**, **Subject**, and **Date** sections in the main reading panel.

How do I collapse the left panel in my AOL Mail Inbox?

Want a bit more room to stretch out and read your email? Well now you can by collapsing the left panel.

Here's how:

1. At the top of your inbox, click the left arrow to collapse the left panel.

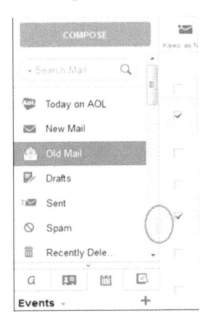

Tada! You'll notice your inbox just got a lot roomier with even more space to read your email. And you can still access all the stuff that was in the left panel by clicking the buttons on the side.

When you want to expand the left panel, just click the right arrow at the top.

Note: You can also move your pointer over the left panel dividing line and click and drag the line to collapse and reopen the left panel.

We hope you enjoy your new roomier inbox!

How do I collapse the lower-left panel in AOL Mail?

The lower-left panel in your AOL Mail inbox gives you quick access to some of the things that you use the most – like your AIM Buddy list, your Contacts, your Calendar, and your To Dos.

However, if you want more room to see your folders, you can collapse this lower panel.

To collapse the lower-left panel:

1. At the top of the lower panel, move your pointer over the dividing bar so you see double arrows.

2. Then click and hold and drag the line all the way to the bottom of your inbox.

That's it! To re-open the panel, just click the feature that you'd like to use.

What is Customize in AOL Mail?

Did you know you can customize the way your messages are displayed in your Inbox? You can adjust the spacing between each message, show a preview of each message, turn the reading pane on (or off), and change the font.

Here's how:

1. Above your list of messages, in the upper right, click the **Customize** button (gear wheel icon).

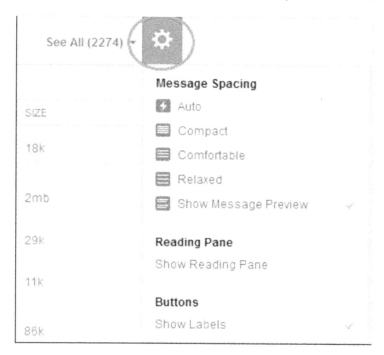

2. Here are some of the things you can do to customize the look of your Inbox.

Message Spacing
Auto – The default amount of space between your messages (you're probably using this setting now!).
Compact – Click **Compact** to compress your message list and see more messages "above the fold".
Comfortable – Click **Comfortable** to slightly compress your message list (not as much as Compact) and move a few more messages into view.
Relaxed – Click **Relaxed** to give more space between each message.
Show Message Preview – This does exactly what you would expect it to do – displays a preview or snippet of each message in your Inbox.

Reading Pane

Click **Show Reading Pane** to turn the reading pane on. The reading pane lets you read an email in the bottom half of your Inbox, while displaying a partial list of your messages in the upper half of your Inbox.

Buttons

You can toggle the labels under the buttons in your AOL Mail Inbox on or off by clicking **Show Labels**.

All these features make customizing your Inbox a snap. Try them out and see which ones you like best!

How do I disable the reading pane?

There are two ways you can disable the reading pane in AOL Mail:

- from the **Customize** drop-down menu above your Inbox OR
- in your **Settings**

Here's how to:

To disable the reading pane from the Customize menu:

1. In the upper right, click the **Customize** button (gear wheel icon), and then under 'Reading Pane', click **Show Reading Pane** to remove the checkmark.

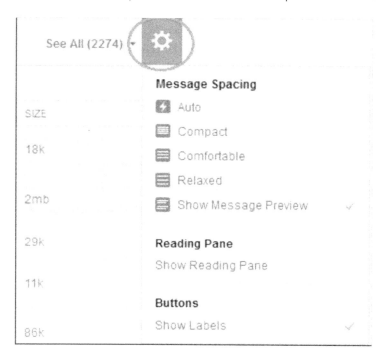

To disable the reading pane in Settings:

1. In the upper right, below your Username, click **Options** and then click **Mail Settings**.

2. On the "General Settings" page, in the **Reading** section, click the box next to **Enable reading pane to preview mail** to remove the check mark.

3. At the bottom of the page, click **Save Settings**. All done!

How do I ensure that new mail is displayed automatically?

Never miss a new email by setting your AOL Mail account to display new mail messages automatically. It's quick, easy, and takes just a few clicks.

To set your new mail messages to be displayed automatically:

1. In the upper right, below your Username, click **Options**, and then click **Mail Settings**.

2. On the General Settings page, in the "New Mail" section, make sure there's a check mark in the box next to **Display new mail automatically**.

3. Scroll to the bottom of the page and click the **Save Settings** button to save the changes.

That's it! Your new email messages will be automatically displayed.

How do I switch between versions of AOL Mail (Basic Version, Accessible Version, and Standard Version)?

AOL Mail is available in three different versions. Here, you can learn how to switch between all the versions of AOL Mail.

- **Standard version** – This is the new version of AOL Mail.

- **Accessibility version** – This is the version of AOL Mail where you can work on the mail box without using a mouse. This version is optimized for users to navigate and perform functions using keyboard shortcuts.
- **Basic version** – This is the older version of AOL Mail.

Switching from Standard version to Accessible version or Basic version

To switch to the Accessible or Basic versions of AOL Mail:

1. Sign in to AOL Mail as you would normally do.

2. In the upper right, below your Username,
click **Options**

3. In the drop-down menu, click on the version of AOL Mail (**Accessible version** or **Basic Version**) that you prefer.

Account Info

Make AOL My Homepage

Mail Settings

Mail Themes

Mobile

Send Us Your Feedback

Help

Visit the Blog

Basic Version

Accessible Version

Download the Mail Toolbar

AOL Terms of Service

AOL Privacy Policy

About Our Ads

Your AOL Mail will change to the version that you have opted for.

Switching back to the Standard version of AOL Mail.

To switch back to the Standard version:

1. Sign in to AOL Mail as you would normally do.

2. In the upper right, below your Username, click **Options**.

3. In the drop-down menu, click **Standard Version**.

Your AOL Mail will change to the Standard version.

Keyboard and Mouse Shortcuts.

What are the mouse shortcuts in AOL Mail?

On AOL Mail, you can use the quick action menu to perform tasks quickly and easily. The quick action menu is available by right-clicking on the Mail and Calendar windows.

Here's the Mail mouse shortcuts:

1. Right-click on any email to access the Quick Action features. You should see a list like the one below.

```
Open in New Window

Reply
Reply All
Forward

Mark Unread
Flag Message
Delete
Report Spam
Show Message Status
Filter messages like this

Search for From/To
Search for Subject

Add to Contacts
Add to Calendar

View Message Source
```

Here's the Calendar mouse shortcuts:

2. Right-click on any calendar event to access the Calendar Quick Action feature. You should see a list like the one below.

```
Edit
Details
Delete

Hide this Calendar
Show this Calendar Only

New Event
```

End of Topic.

A fresh topic

AOL Mail: Troubleshooting.

Learn what to do if you have trouble with your AOL Mail. Get help if you have problems signing in or sending and receiving mail.

Trouble Signing In.

Use the following solutions if you're having trouble signing into your AOL Mail account.

I'm having trouble signing in to my account

Why do I get a blank screen when trying to sign in to AOL Mail?

There are several reasons why your screen is blank when signing in to AOL Mail. Don't worry, AOL team are here to help!

Try the solutions below, checking to see if you can access your mail after each solution, until the problem is fixed.

Solutions.

Sign out and then sign back in

Sometimes, the best solution is also the easiest. If you're having trouble accessing your mail, sign out of your account, wait a few minutes, and then sign back in. This will often do the trick.

Clear browser cache, cookies and history

When you visit a website, temporary Internet files, cookies, and your browsing history are stored on your computer to record your return visit. Deleting these files (Internet files, cookies, and browsing history) can often fix the problem you're experiencing.

The instructions to clear your cache, cookies, and footprints will differ depending on the browser you use.

Reset web settings

Try to access your AOL Mail using a different browser

Try accessing your mail using a different web browser. Open the new browser and go to mail.aol.com and sign in with your AOL Username and password. If you still receive the error message, please wait a few minutes and then try again.

If you're using a firewall, allow the following friendly URLs

If you're using a firewall, allow the following friendly URLs: (*.aol.com, *.aim.com, registration.aol.com, webmail.aol.com, and mail.aol.com). For additional support configuring third party firewalls, please contact the firewall manufacturer.

In order to address this issue, please disable your pop-up blocking software. Alternatively, you could add a web site such as AOL.com to the "white list" of domains accepted by your pop-up blocker software. If you are unsure how to disable your pop-up blocking software or add a domain to the"white list", please contact the vendor of your pop-up blocking software for assistance or simply reference the Help guide included with your software.

Most pop-up blockers also allow you to hold down the Shift key as you click web site links. This disables pop-up blocking on a one-time basis.

Check if Java Applet Scripting and cookies are enabled in Internet Options

My AOL Mail sign in screen is missing

Something missing? If you can't see the AOL Mail sign in screen, try the solutions below to fix the problem, checking whether you can see the sign in screen after each solution.

Solutions.

Reset web settings

If you've installed multiple web browsers, some of your browser settings may have changed. However, you can reset your web settings without changing the settings of other browsers on your computer. Please visit this help article <u>Reset web settings</u> and select your browser version to learn how to set your web settings to default.

Clear cookies, cache, history and footprints

When you visit a website, temporary internet files, your browsing history, and cookies are stored on your computer to record your return visit. Deleting these files can fix the problem you're experiencing.

Problems Receiving or Reading Mail.

Use the following solutions if you're having trouble reading or receiving mail. Select a heading below to expand more information.

Why am I not able to read email in AOL Mail?

There could be many different reasons why you're not able to read your email in AOL Mail. But don't worry, AOL team are here to help!

Below are some solutions to resolve the issue. After trying the first solution, check whether you can read your email. If you still can't read your mail, continue to the next solution - checking after each solution to see if you can read your email - until you are able to do so.

Solutions.

Clear cookies, cache, history, and footprints

When you visit a website, temporary Internet files and cookies are stored on your computer to record your return visit. Sometimes, these temporary Internet files and cookies can cause the issue that you're currently experiencing. Similarly, your history list can also be a concern.

Reset web settings

If you've installed multiple web browsers, some of your browser settings may have changed. However, you can reset your web settings without changing the settings of other browsers on your computer.

Disable the pop-up blocking software

1. Try to access your AOL Mail using a different browser like Mozilla Firefox or Chrome.

2. Try to access your AOL Mail using a different computer (ideally from a different location).

Note: Most pop-up blockers also allow you to hold down the Shift key as you click website links. This disables pop-up blocking on a one-time basis.

Disable the pop-up window in the AOL Mail settings

1. Open AOL Mail.

2. Click **Options** and select **Settings**.

3. Select the **General** tab.

4. In the **Pop-Up Windows** section, make sure "**Always read mail in a new window**" and "**Always write mail in a new window**" are not checked. If checked, uncheck and click **Save Settings**.

Note: In the **General** tab under **Reading**, make sure "**Enable reading pane to preview mail**" is checked.

Temporarily disable a firewall or configure McAfee

There may be a firewall or other security software on your computer that is preventing you from connecting to the

AOL service. You can temporarily disable your firewall and check whether you are able to connect to the Internet.

Disable Internet Protected Mode in Internet Explorer

Protected Mode is ON by default in recent versions of Internet Explorer. It can interfere with Mail. If you're having trouble reading mail in Internet Explorer, try turning Protected Mode OFF. Here's how:

Open the **Tools** menu, go to **Internet Options**, and click or tap the **Security** tab. Toward the bottom of the window, **un-check** "Enable Protected Mode". To complete the change, restart Internet Explorer then load AOL Mail.

Try accessing your mailbox using AOL Mail Basic Version

AOL Mail Basic Version is a quick way to see your email and is great when you've got a slower connection speed. Please click the following link to connect to BasicVersion: AOL Mail: Basic Version

Why can't I view pictures in AOL Mail?

Having trouble viewing pictures in AOL Mail? Try the solutions below, checking to see if you can view pictures in your mail after each solution.

Solutions.

Clear cookies, cache, history, and footprints

When you visit a website, temporary Internet files and cookies are stored on your computer to record your return visit. Sometimes, these temporary Internet files and cookies can cause the issue that you're currently experiencing. Clearing your cookies, cache, and history can often fix the problem.

Reset web settings

If you've installed multiple web browsers, some of your browser settings may have changed. However, you can reset your web settings without changing the settings of other browsers on your computer. Please visit this help article <u>Reset web settings</u> and select your browser version to learn how to set your web settings to default.

Check for attachments

The picture may have been sent as an attachment rather than being embedded in the mail.

To check if the picture is an attachment, in the header of the email, under the username of the person who sent you the email, you would see a paper clip icon followed by the name of the file (picture).

Note: If the picture is an attachment, you'll need to download the attachment to view the picture.

Try again later

The problem could be caused by a lot of people accessing their mail at the same time, which can lead to delays or slow responses. If this seems to be the case, please hang tight for a few minutes, and then try accessing your email again.

Note: If the picture was embedded using another file format, such as TIFF, you may not be able to view it. Please ask the sender to resend the picture using the JPG or GIF file format.

I don't receive the emails I sent to myself

There are a few reasons why you may not be getting email that you've sent to yourself.

It could be because:

One of your filters could be directing the email into a folder

If you've set up filters, the message you sent yourself might be going directly to a different folder than your Inbox. Here's how to check your filters:

1. In the upper right, under your Username, click **Options**, and then click **Mail Settings**.

2. In the left panel, click **Filters and Alerts**.

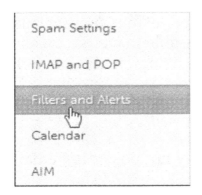

3. Do you see a filter that might be capturing the mail you've been looking for? If yes, move your pointer over the filter and then click the **X** button next to Edit.

Priority	Filter Name		Criteria and Actions
1	New Filter	Edit ✕	Find: From: johndoeusername Do: Move to folder: Friends

There's a delay in delivery

Messages are usually delivered right away. Very rarely, there is a delay while in transit. This is usually due to problems on the mail server, heavy internet traffic, or routing problems. Unfortunately, aside from waiting, there's no way to know whether a message has been delayed or whether it has been rendered undeliverable. If a sender can re-send it, have them do that.

Why can't I retrieve my mail?

If you're having trouble getting your email in AOL Mail, try the solutions below, checking after each solution to see if the problem is fixed.

Solutions.

Log out, then log back into AOL Mail

Enable Java applet scripting and cookies

Enabling Java applet scripting and cookies may help you fix the problem. To learn how to enable Java applet scripting and cookies, please visit this help article <u>Enable Java applet scripting and cookies</u>.

Clear cookies, cache, history, and footprints

When you visit a website, temporary Internet files and cookies are stored on your computer to record your return visit. Sometimes, these temporary Internet files and cookies can cause the issue that you're currently experiencing. Clearing your cookies, cache, and history can often fix the problem.

Reset web settings

If you've installed multiple web browsers, some of your browser settings may have changed. However, you can reset your web settings without changing the settings of other browsers on your computer. Please visit this help article <u>Reset web settings</u> and select your browser version to learn how to set your web settings to default.

Why am I unable to receive emails from specific senders?

If you're unable to receive emails from specific senders on AOL Mail, try the solutions listed below. After trying the first solution, check if the issue is resolved. If it isn't, continue to the next solutions until the issue is resolved.

Check your spam folder

The email may have accidentally been delivered to your **Spam** folder.

1. In the left panel, click **Spam**.

2. If you find the email that you're looking for, click the box next to it, and then above your messages, click **OK NOT SPAM**.

Note: When you click **OK NOT SPAM**, the email returns to your Inbox and is listed under the date you originally received the message.

Add the specific sender to your contacts list to ensure that his/her mail is delivered to your Inbox.

Additional Troubleshooting for Domain Admins/Email Service Providers

If you're still not able to receive emails sent from a specific sender, please request the sender's email service provider to contact AOL Postmaster.

How can I find emails that are missing from my AOL Mail Inbox?

If it looks like you're missing emails that were previously in your AOL Mail Inbox, here are a handful of solutions that'll help you find them.

IMPORTANT: If you have a free account with AOL and you haven't accessed your account in the last 90 days, any email associated with that account will be deleted per AOL's Terms of Service. The next time you sign in, you'll have a new, clean mailbox ready to use. We (AOL team) apologize for any inconvenience. If you have a paid account or you frequently access your emails, don't worry: Your email experience will remain unchanged.

Note: The number of days an email stays in your mailbox depends on the type of mailbox you use and the folder in which you saved the email.

You access your email using an email client (like Microsoft Outlook) or on your mobile device

Do you check your AOL Mail using another email account or program? This is perhaps the top reason people don't find email where they think it should be. If you "POP" your mail into another account or program, chances are that the settings *in that program* are actually set to delete the mail from the AOL server each time you check your mail. The fix? Go into that program's POP/IMAP settings and find the option to "Leave messages on server," and select it.

Alternatively, if your email isn't *missing* but is going straight into the **Old**, **Recently Deleted** or **Trash** folders, this may simply be the normal outcome of using IMAP to access your AOL Mail in another program or on another device. IMAP syncs your mail regardless of where you use it, which means if you read a message in your mailbox on your mobile device, it will appear as "Read" the next time you check your mail from anywhere else.

Check the Trash folder

If the email was accidentally deleted from your inbox, you might be able to recover it from the **Trash** folder.

To check the Trash folder:

1. In the left panel, click the **Trash** folder.

2. Determine whether the message that you're looking for is in this folder.

3. If you find the email in your **Trash** folder you can still restore it. Click the box next to the email, click the **Action** drop-down menu, and then under "Move To", click where you'd like to move the message to.

Check the Saved Mail folder

The email may have been saved in the **Saved Mail** folder.

To check the Saved Mail folder:

1. In the left panel, click **My Folders**.

2. Click the **Saved Mail** folder.

3. Check if the missing email is in this folder.

Check the Spam Folder

The email may have been accidentally diverted to your **Spam** folder.

To check the Spam folder:

1. In the left panel, click **Spam**.

2. Determine whether the email that you're looking for is in this folder. If you find the email in the Spam folder and would like to move it to your Inbox, check the box next to the message, and then above your list of messages, click **OK NOT SPAM**.

Note: When you click **OK NOT SPAM**, the email will return to your Inbox and will be listed by the date that it was originally received.

Delete incoming mail filter

An incoming mail filter could be delivering messages to a particular folder instead of your inbox.

To delete an incoming mail filter:

1. In the upper right, under your Username, click **Options** and then click **Settings**.

2. In the left panel, click **Filters and Alerts**.

3. Move your pointer over the filter that you'd like to delete and click the white **X** in the box to the right of **Edit**.

4. At the bottom of your screen you'll see a confirmation that the filter has been deleted. Delete the wrong filter? No

problem. Click the **Undo** link on the right to restore the filter.

Check if your account has been compromised

Sometimes, missing emails are an indication that your account has been hacked. To learn how to identify a compromised or hacked account, please visit this AOL help article <u>Account Management: Identifying suspicious activity</u>.

Does my AOL Mail account get deactivated if I don't use it for 90 days?

Yes, an AOL Mail account does get deactivated if it is inactive for more than 90 days. To keep your account active, please sign in to your account at least once every 90 days.

Why is AOL Mail temporarily unavailable?

You may receive the message "Email is temporarily unavailable" or "Mail is not available" because of various factors, including network traffic, system issues, or maintenance. These are system-generated errors. It's also possible that some adjustments are being made in the area where you live.

The best thing to do is wait a few minutes, and then try accessing your email again. If you still can't access your mail, the solutions may help you resolve this issue:

- **Switch to AOL WebMail Basic version**: If your mail does not load, you can use the basic version of

The email may have been accidentally diverted to your **Spam** folder.

To check the Spam folder:

1. In the left panel, click **Spam**.

2. Determine whether the email that you're looking for is in this folder. If you find the email in the Spam folder and would like to move it to your Inbox, check the box next to the message, and then above your list of messages, click **OK NOT SPAM**.

Note: When you click **OK NOT SPAM**, the email will return to your Inbox and will be listed by the date that it was originally received.

Delete incoming mail filter

An incoming mail filter could be delivering messages to a particular folder instead of your inbox.

To delete an incoming mail filter:

1. In the upper right, under your Username, click **Options** and then click **Settings**.

2. In the left panel, click **Filters and Alerts**.

3. Move your pointer over the filter that you'd like to delete and click the white **X** in the box to the right of **Edit**.

4. At the bottom of your screen you'll see a confirmation that the filter has been deleted. Delete the wrong filter? No

problem. Click the **Undo** link on the right to restore the filter.

Check if your account has been compromised

Sometimes, missing emails are an indication that your account has been hacked. To learn how to identify a compromised or hacked account, please visit this AOL help article <u>Account Management: Identifying suspicious activity</u>.

Does my AOL Mail account get deactivated if I don't use it for 90 days?

Yes, an AOL Mail account does get deactivated if it is inactive for more than 90 days. To keep your account active, please sign in to your account at least once every 90 days.

Why is AOL Mail temporarily unavailable?

You may receive the message "Email is temporarily unavailable" or "Mail is not available" because of various factors, including network traffic, system issues, or maintenance. These are system-generated errors. It's also possible that some adjustments are being made in the area where you live.

The best thing to do is wait a few minutes, and then try accessing your email again. If you still can't access your mail, the solutions may help you resolve this issue:

- **Switch to AOL WebMail Basic version**: If your mail does not load, you can use the basic version of

AOL WebMail, which is available at http://basic.webmail.aol.com/.

Problems Sending or Composing Mail.

Use the following solutions to help resolve the issues with sending or composing mail.

I'm unable to send email

Can't send email with AOL Mail? If you have a problem sending mail, try these options in the order they are listed. After each one, take a look to check if you can send before trying the next option.

You might want to print a copy of these instructions, or make sure the page is open in a separate browser window as you go through the suggested steps.

Information you need.

You will need to know the version of the Microsoft Windows operating system and the Internet Explorer browser installed on your computer. You can find this information by following the instructions given in the online help articles mentioned below:

- Determining your version of Microsoft Windows
- How do I determine the version of Internet Explorer I have?

Solutions.

Clear cookies, cache, history, and footprints

Disable the pop-up blocking software

Restart the computer

Use a different browser

Enable/disable firewall using McAfee Internet Security Suite - Special edition from AOL

Why won't images show when forwarded through AOL Mail?

The recipient of your email may not be able to view the picture in the email you forwarded through AOL Mail if you are sending email in plain text, or if you're using the Mac Safari™ browser. After trying the solution, check to see if the recipient of your email can view the picture in the email you sent. If they are still unable to view the picture in the email you sent, continue using the suggested solutions until the problem is fixed.

Enable Rich Text/HTML:

If your Compose Settings are not set to use rich text or HTML, images will not be seen in forwarded emails.

1. In the upper right, below your Username, click the **Options** drop-down menu, and then click **Mail Settings**.

2. In the left panel, click **Compose**.

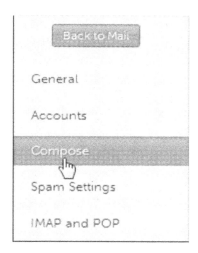

3. Click the box next to **Use Rich Text/HTML Editing** to place a check mark in it.

4. Scroll to the bottom of the page and click **Save**.

Note: You can also enable this feature by clicking the **Enable rich text editor** button, in the compose mail window.

Download the Attachment, Then Resend the Image as an Attachment:

You may need to save the attachment to your computer and then send the image with a new email.

1. Open the email which has attachments, then click the attached file.

2. On the **File Download** window, click the **Save** button.

3. On the **Save As** window, navigate to the folder where you want to save the image, then click the **Save** button.

4. On the **Download complete** window, click the **Close** button.

5. In the upper right of the email with attachment, click the **X** button to close it.

6. Click the **Compose** button.

7. In the **To:** box, type the Username or email address of the person to whom you want to send the image.

8. To attach the file, click the **paper clip** icon.

9. Navigate to the folder with the image you want to attach, click the file name to highlight it, then click the **Open** button.

Note: Repeat the last two steps for each image you want to attach.

10. When you're ready to send your message, click the **Send** button at the top.

My Sent folder or outbox contains emails that I didn't send

Are your contacts getting emails that you didn't send? Is your Sent folder (or any other folder) suddenly empty or missing?

If so, your account has most likely been hacked (or compromised) and has been accessed by someone other than you. It usually means someone figured out your password.

Check for these signs:

- Your inbox is full of MAILER-DAEMON rejection notices for messages you didn't send.
- People you know are getting emails from you that you didn't send.
- There are outgoing messages in your Sent, Drafts or Outbox folder that you didn't create or send.
- Your account folders (Sent, Deleted, Spam, Inbox, etc.) have been emptied or deleted.
- Your Address Book contacts have been erased.
- During sign-in or when sending a message, you're asked to pass an image challenge.
- Emails you try to send are suddenly getting refused and returned to you.
- There are contacts in your Address Book you didn't add.

- You keep getting bumped offline when you're signed into your account.
- Your Display Name has been changed or looks odd.
- Your email signature suddenly has a link you didn't put there.
- You're not getting new mail, OR your new mail is going straight into your Saved IMs folder.

If you think your account has been hacked, you should:

- Go to i.aol.com to change your password. **Note:** The new password should be at least eight characters long and include at least one number, letter (combination of upper and lower cases) and special character ($, *, &, !, etc.). Also, if you used the same password for other online accounts such as social media and financial services, change those passwords as well. Make sure these new passwords are very different from your new AOL Mail password.

If you can't sign on with your current password...

When an email account suddenly appears tied to suspicious activity, we (AOL team) place a temporary hold on the account. You can access your account again by changing your password..

Note: If you still can't change your password or security question (ASQ) after visiting i.aol.com, please call 1-855-622-4946 (Mon-Fri 8am-1am ET and Sat-Sun 8am-10pm ET) and we (AOL team) will be more than happy to help you.

To help keep your account safe, we (AOL Mail team) **recommend that you:**

- **Learn to spot phishing email scams.** Please visit the <u>AOL Account Security site</u> for more information on how to best protect your account, how to spot a phishing email, and what you should do when you receive one.
- **Protect your account with comprehensive online security.** You can download software to help protect your computer from viruses, spyware, hackers and even identity theft. For more information regarding safety and security for your PC, please visit *AOL Internet Security Central.*
- **Keep tabs on your account.** Periodically check the Usernames on your account by going to i.aol.com. If you see a Username you don't recognize, select it and click delete. If you're missing a Username that you formerly had under your account, you can restore it by clicking Restore a Recently Deleted Screen Name from the main Screen Names menu. Check each Username's profile to make sure it hasn't been changed.
- **Recognize AOL Certified emails.** Email coming from AOL is often sent as "Certified Mail," which means it's marked with a unique green ribbon icon. This icon is visible from your inbox view before you open the email to help you identify authentic AOL messages.

REMEMBER: AOL employees will never ask you for your password.

Why am I getting an image challenge when trying to send mail?

If you're seeing an image challenge when trying to send mail, entering the image in the box should do the trick. However, if you correctly enter the image challenge and still can't send mail, it may be signs of a more serious issue with your account.

End of Topic.

A fresh topic

Accessibility and Keyboard Shortcuts for AOL Mail.

Learn about accessibility and keyboard shortcuts for AOL Mail

In the Internet Explorer and Firefox browsers, press the ALT key along with the letter listed below. In Safari, press the CTRL or Apple key along with the letter listed below. For example: To write a new email in Internet Explorer, press and hold the ALT key, then press the W key.

Use the following list of keyboard shortcuts to enhance your productivity in AOL.

Keyboard Shortcuts in the Email Window on AOL Mail.

In the **Email** window:

Action	Shortcut
Write Email	W
Next Page	N
Previous Page	P
Show/Hide Search	F

Keyboard Shortcuts in the Write Email Window on AOL Mail.

In the **Write Email** window:

Action	Shortcut
Opens People Picker in the To: field	T
Opens People Picker in the Cc: field	C
Opens People Picker in the Bcc: field	B
Spell Check	=
Next Page (in People Picker)	N
Previous Page (in People Picker)	P

Keyboard Shortcuts in the Read Email Window on AOL Mail.

In the **Read Email** window:

Action	Shortcut
Reply	R
Reply All	A
Forward	F
Delete	D
Next Message	N
Previous Message	P
Print	T

Keyboard Shortcuts in AOL Calendar on AOL Mail.

In the **Calendar** window:

Action	Shortcut
Add event/task	A
Month view	M
Week view	W
Day view	D
Event list	E
Tasks	T
Next month/week/day/page	N
Previous month/week/day/page	P

Show/hide search	F

Keyboard Shortcuts in Quick Action or Right-click Menu on AOL Mail.

Within the **Quick Actions** or **Right-Click** menu:

Action	Shortcut
Search for "Subject"	S
Reply	R
Reply All	A
Forward	F
Delete	D
Keep as New (Note: On AIM/Netscape: Mark as Unread)	**K**
Add to Calendar	**C**
Add to Tasks	**T**

Note: In the Quick Actions or Right-Click menu, no **Alt** key is needed, simply use the letter key.

Limitations of AOL Mail

The new version of the AOL.com service has not yet been optimised for the following:

- members of the disability community
- some non-English languages
- some older operating systems and browsers

If you run into these issues, the older version of the AOL.com service can still be used by going here http://mail.aol.com/en-gb/lite.

CHAPTER 10.

Tips, Tricks, Techniques, and Keyboard Shortcuts for use in Yandex mail.

Introduction: This refers to the free email service provision by the Russian Multinational technology company called Yandex.

A fresh topic

What to Know About Yandex Mail.

Unlimited

You will receive a 10 GB mailbox after <u>registration</u>. If you use the Mail web interface regularly, the mailbox size automatically increases by 1 GB as soon as there is less than 200 MB of free space.

Personal

You can select a theme for your Mail. Install the theme you like or enable a three-pane page view.

Convenient

You can group your messages by topics, add labels, configure personal buttons, and use hot keys. Documents, archives, images, and media files that you receive can be viewed or listened to directly in Mail, without installing any additional programs.

Reliable protection against spam and viruses

Yandex uses proprietary technologies to fight spam and continuously improves algorithms for recognition of unsolicited messages. All incoming messages are checked by Dr.Web antivirus and virus-infected mail is blocked by the Yandex mail server.

Mobile

Yandex.Mail's mobile application "" allows you to not only work with email, but also exchange instant messages and send coordinates of your current whereabouts or the location of upcoming meetings.

End of Topic.

A fresh topic

Solutions to Problems.

Solutions to some problems that you may face when using Yandex.Mail are listed below.

Yandex.Mail does not Load or is not Working Correctly.

If you face problems when working with Mail, for example, the mailbox takes too long to load, some actions cannot be performed, or you are prompted to use a light version of Mail, may be caused by:

- using outdated browsers which do not meet modern security and performance requirements;
- data loss during transfer from Yandex servers to your computer.

To eliminate possible causes, please install the latest version of your browser. Also make sure you are using a secure HTTPS connection.

If Internet Explorer continues working incorrectly after the update, it may be due to several causes. The most widespread problems and troubleshooting tips are listed below.

ActiveX is disabled in the browser

XML and XSL page element processing plug-ins are disabled in the browser

The wrong compatibility mode is selected in Internet Explorer 8 and higher

If your antivirus is configured to check HTTPS connections, this may cause the following problems in some situations:

- the contents of the Mail page do not load or are displayed incorrectly (styles and executable scripts do not load);
- When downloading a page, some errors occur related to the security certificate.

To resolve the problem, disable verification and clear the browser cache.

Messages Disappear from my Mailbox.

If emails disappeared from the **Inbox**, they were probably moved to the **Deleted**, **Spam** or other folder. If you remember the name or the address of the sender, a part of the message wording or the subject, try to look for the email in all the folders in your mailbox.

Restoring emails from the Deleted folder

Attention! If the missing emails are not found in **Deleted**, it is possible that a month has elapsed since they were moved to **Deleted** and the **Deleted** folder was emptied automatically. Therefore, such emails cannot be restored.

If the emails were moved from the **Inbox** folder to the **Deleted** folder less than one month ago, they can be restored. To do this, go to the **Deleted** folder, select the required emails, click on **Move to folder** and select the required folder from the list.

Why do emails go to Deleted and how can it be avoided

The other mail service is set up for the collection of emails from your Yandex mailbox

> If you have a mailbox from another mail service which has a mail fetcher configured for the collection of emails from your Yandex mailbox, the emails on Yandex.Mail will be automatically moved to the **Deleted** folder. To resolve the problem, disable the mail fetcher on the other mail service and configure Yandex.Mail to forward emails to a different email-address by enabling the option **save a copy when forwarding**.

A message deleting rule has been configured.

> Make sure the mail processing rules are not configured to delete incoming mail. If there are any, try to disable them temporarily and see whether messages will be received in the **Inbox**.

Another user has access to your mailbox

> Emails can be deleted by a user who, for some reason, has access to your mailbox: you may have forgotten to close your session on somebody else's device. To close the session, click **Log out on all devices** in the account menu. You can also do this on the page Passports from the link **Log out on all computers**.

> Go to the session history log and check for any delete email operations.

Restriction. The log stores about 2000 operations. If more than 2000 actions were performed after deleting emails, data on the delete operation will not be displayed in the log.

If you are sure that only you have access to your mailbox, test your computer with an antivirus software, change the password and additional address. Also check if there are any unknown numbers on the Phone numbers page.

Internet Scams (Phishing).

Phishing consists of a variety of Internet scams that are designed to collect confidential user information (account passwords, credit card numbers, PINs, etc.).

Frauds use mass mailings on behalf of companies, services, and social networks to send notifications about events which require users to submit, update, or confirm their confidential information.

Examples of these types of events include:

- **Confirmation of account information, delivery problems, or system failures.** The message asks you to provide your username and password for this service or website. Most often, the **From** field of these types of messages contains **Customer Support** or **admin**. Yandex staff members and Support will never ask you to send your login information.
- **Identity verification and mailbox activation.** You will be asked to send a SMS to a short number.

SMS messages to short numbers usually costs more than other SMS under your rate plan, but information about this inflated cost is usually withheld or given in a part of the message where it is least visible. As a result, an arbitrary amount, most often 100–200 rubles, is debited from your phone account right after the message is sent to the short number. In a number of situations, a feature debiting daily funds from your phone account may be enabled. Be cautious: Yandex will never ask you to send SMS. Instead, it sends SMS to you. You do not need to answer these SMS.

- **Participation in prize drawings.** Here, you will be prompted to fill in a form where you need to provide your full name and contact phone numbers, as well as your passport information and a credit card number. If you receive a message about Yandex holds a drawing for prizes, contact Yandex team by using details on http//company.yandex.ru/contacts and get more specific information. If there is a drawing, make sure you are not asked to pay for the prize delivery in advance or pay a participation fee, because Yandex never offers to pay for what you yourself have not ordered.
- A phishing message may include a **link that takes you to a page on a fake website**. Scam artists easily get access to the details entered by the user on these types of pages. When logging into Yandex, make sure the website address looks exactly like this name.yandex.ru/section. Yandex.ru must be followed by / rather than a period.

Carefully view all incoming mail and check link addresses so as not to fall victim to phishing scams. Phishing links often contain a meaningless combination of characters or typos. Never pay for purchases or bills you are not sure about; never send SMS to suspicious numbers; and never give your Yandex password to anyone.

If you discover a phishing message or a suspicious email, please, inform Yandex team by using the feedback form and attach its properties. After that there will be a warning on this email:

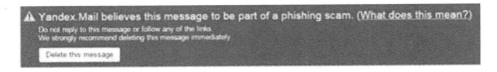

What should you do if you fall victim to fraud

- Contact the police department if funds have been unlawfully debited from your account.
- If you followed a phishing link, check your computer for viruses with free anti-virus programs such as CureIt! from Dr. Web and Virus Removal Tool from "Kaspersky Lab".
- If you have entered your password on a fake page, definitely change it in Passport and change your security question and answer. This information should be changed after a virus check. If you have lost access to your account, follow instructions on restoring access.

Emails are not reaching my mailbox

If you have not received a message or notification, make sure that:

- you have entered the correct address on the website sending correspondence, and the sender has entered the correct address;
- the message is not in **Spam**. If this has occurred, click **Not spam!** to move the message to the **Inbox**.

Message delivery problems may also occur because of technical problems on the mail servers of the sender or recipient, heavy traffic in communication channels, etc. In this case, the sender will receive an automatic report stating the reason for nondelivery.

If the sender does not receive a report listing the reason the message was not delivered, then the problem lies with the sender's mail server.

A message from Yandex was rejected by the mail server.

If you have sent a message from your Yandex mailbox but it has been rejected by the recipient's mail server, you will get an automatic report from "Mailer-Daemon" with reasons for non-delivery and the name of the server which rejected passing the message to its destination.

Note. You can review a list of possible reasons why messages you sent to a Yandex mailbox from another mail server are rejected by the Yandex mail server, in this article Message bounced by Yandex.Mail.

Wrong address of the recipient

The recipient's mailbox is full

The recipient's address is blocked by his or her mail service

The recipient's mail server does not accept large messages

The recipient's mail server treats emails as spam

Yandex mail server is blacklisted

A "loop" was detected in sent messages

Forwarding prohibited

Error verifying the sender

Message Bounced by Yandex.Mail

If you have sent a message to a Yandex mailbox which has been rejected by Yandex mail server, you will receive an automatic report from "Mailer-Daemon" with reasons for non-delivery and the name of the server which rejected further passage of the message to its destination.

Note. If you have sent the message from your Yandex mailbox and it has been rejected by the recipient's mail server, you can view a list of possible causes in the article <u>A message from Yandex was rejected by the mail server.</u>.

No such user

If the report contains the following strings, the message has been sent to a non-existing address:

- "No such user"
- "No correct recipients"
- "Bad recipient address syntax"

- "Bad address mailbox syntax"
- "Recipient address rejected: need fully-qualified address"

Make sure the recipient's address does not include extra punctuation marks, spaces, or quotation marks. Confirm the recipient's email address and resend the message.

Message rejected under suspicion of SPAM

If the report contains the string "Message rejected under suspicion of SPAM", the contents of your message were recognized by "Anti-Spam" as spam.

If only spam is coming from your mailbox, Yandex mail server will block receipt of messages from it for 24 hours. In this case, the non-delivery report will contain the following string"Client host [<IP_host>] blocked using spamsource.mail.yandex.net; see..." или "Blocked by spam statistics — see...".

If you are sure that your computer is not infected with a virus and has not been used to distribute spam, report this to Yandex.Mail Support through the feedback form by attaching the message file with the report.

Note. If you are sending legitimate messages to your website users or subscribers, please read <u>Yandex requirements for honest mailing lists</u>.

Error: too many recipients

If there is the following string in the report: "Error: too many recipients", your email has too many recipients:

more than 35 addresses in fields **To**, **Cc** and **Bcc**. Edit the list of recipients and try again.

Message size exceeds fixed limit (Error: message file too big)

If the report contains the string "Error: message file too big" or "Message size exceeds fixed limit", the attachment you are sending in the message cannot be accepted by Yandex mail server because of size limitations.

The maximum size of messages with attachments that can be sent to Yandex mailboxes is 30 MB.

Message infected by virus

If the report contains the string "Message infected by virus", your message has been marked by Yandex mail server as being infected by a virus.

Target address blocked due to policy violation

If the report contains the string: "Policy rejection on the target address", it means that the account of your email recipient was blocked due to a violation of the <u>user agreement</u>. Try to contact the recipient by an alternate means of communication to report the problem.

If you are the owner of the address to which the message has been sent, you can unblock it yourself. Fill in appropriate information about yourself on Modify personal information and go through the unblocking procedure.

The recipient has exceeded their message rate limit. Try again later

If the report contains the string "The recipient has exceeded their message rate limit. Try again later", message delivery to the recipient's address has been suspended due to a large number of messages received by his/her mailbox at the current time. Try to send the message again in 24 hours.

Mailbox size exceeded

If the report contains the string "Mailbox size exceeded", the recipient's mailbox has no space left to accept your message. Try to contact the recipient by an alternate means of communication to report the problem.

Error: timeout exceeded

If the report contains the string "Error: timeout exceeded", your mail server has taken too long to respond to system commands and Yandex mail server has terminated the attempt to establish a connection and deliver the message. Try to contact your mail service administration by an alternate means of communication to report the problem.

Error: too many connections

If the report contains the string "Error: too many connections", your mail server has currently created a large number of requests to the Yandex mail server. This increases load and slows down the system. Try to contact your mail service administration by an alternate means of communication to report the problem.

EHLO requires domain address (HELO requires domain address)

If the report contains the string "EHLO requires domain address" or "HELO requires domain address", your mail server incorrectly provided its name when attempting to deliver the message. This error may be returned when invalid characters are used in the system name of the sender's computer in accordance with RFC 2821 and RFC 1045 standards.

Contact your system administrator to resolve this problem.

Other system errors

The non-delivery report may also contain strings such as:

- 501 5.5.4 "Syntax: MAIL FROM: *address*"— misconfigured sequence in mail from
- 501 5.5.4 "Wrong param" — an incorrect parameter
- 502 5.5.2 "Syntax error, command unrecognized" — a command set incorrectly

Try to contact your mail service administration by an alternate means of communication to report the problem.

Email Client Doesn't Work.

If your mail program does not work properly or error messages appear, the following causes may be to blame:

No connection with the server

If you receive a message that there is no connection with the server, try reentering your username and password in the web interface.

Make sure that the protocol you want to use is checked in Email clients.

Make sure the settings of your mail program are configured exactly as given below:

- for POP3 addresses pop.yandex.ru and port 995 with SSL
- for IMAP addresses imap.yandex.ru and port 993 with SSL
- for SMTP addresses smtp.yandex.ru and port 465 with SSL

See <u>Encryption of transmitted data</u> for more details about how to check server settings in different email clients.

Authentication for sending emails is disabled on the Yandex mail server

If you receive the message "Authentication required", "Sender address rejected: Access denied" or "Send auth command first", authorization at Yandex SMTP server is disabled in the settings of the mail program. Make sure **My server requires authentication** (for Outlook Express) or **SMTP Authentication** (for The Bat!) is checked.

Wrong sender address

If you receive the message "Sender address rejected: not owned by auth user", the address you are trying to send a message from does not match the username under which you are authenticated at the SMTP server. Make sure the mail program's reply-to address is configured to the address the username of which is used in SMTP authorization settings.

No access via POP3 protocol

If you receive the message "Username failure or POP3 disabled", the mail program cannot access the mailbox over POP3. Make sure you have entered the right password for your mailbox and POP3 access is enabled on the settings page.

Yandex mail server treats messages as spam

If you receive "Message rejected under suspicion of SPAM", the contents of your email were recognized by Anti-Spam as spam. Contact Yandex.Mail Support through the feedback form to find out the cause of the problem.

Please, also check your computer for viruses with free anti-virus programs such as CureIt! from Dr. Web and Virus Removal Tool from "Kaspersky Lab".

Use Yandex.Mail web interface to send an email.

Messages are copied on the server when deleted/moved using IMAP

Message copying during the movement or deletion over IMAP is based on special features of the IMAP protocol and synchronization settings of email clients. In this event, folders should be forced to synchronize with the server so that the data matches after the actions are performed. In Mozilla Thunderbird, the **Compact** function must be used.

A non-delivery report is received after sending the message

The report always refers to the cause for non-delivery. See <u>Yandex message rejected by the mail server</u> for the most common causes.

I get errors during the SSL activation in the mail client.

If during the activation of SSL-encryption you get errors about an incorrect certificate, make sure that the mail client and the operating system are configured correctly:

- The correct time (without any delays and "dates from the future") is set on the computer. If a wrong date is set, the system erroneously defines the certificate period as not yet started or already elapsed.
- All updates of the operating system are installed.
- Checking of the HTTPS-connections is disabled in the settings of your antivirus software.

Add the certificate to the list of trusted certificates manually (Windows)
Adding the root certificate to Linux

MS Outlook 2007 does not identify the certificate

Problems with confirmation of the certificate in The Bat!

Reconfiguration of your send script fails

1C software does not support SSL

I send emails from a scanner which does not support SSL

I get errors during SSL activation in the jabber-client.

If during the activation of the SSL-encoding in the jabber-client you get errors about the incorrect certificate, change the encoding type in the program settings to **TLS**.

Forwarding mail to another address does not work.

If you have any problems with automatic forwarding of messages to other addresses, please check the <u>Mail processing rules</u> page to confirm that the required rule is enabled and that the address to which the message should be sent is also correct.

Check for any wrong characters in the address you entered.

Also check if the receiving mailbox has any rules deleting or moving messages to **Spam**.

Yandex.Mail search does not work.

If Yandex.Mail search does not work correctly, please write to Yandex.Mail Support through the <u>feedback form</u>. Make sure to list in the message all requirements and conditions for which the search function fails to find emails and also attach the properties of these emails.

A message rule does not work.

After you have set up a message rule, wait a few minutes because it may not work immediately. Also try to replace "matches" with "contains" in the rule conditions.

If the rule does not work a few minutes later and changing the settings does not help, please contact Yandex.Mail Support through the feedback form. Please, describe In the message the rule that did not work and attach the email properties that were to be covered by the conditions of this rule.

The blacklist does not work.

If the blacklist does not work correctly and messages from blacklisted senders continue arriving in your mailbox, please write to Yandex.Mail Support through the feedback form. Make sure to attach the properties of these emails to the message.

The message or attached file does not open

If you have problem reading a message (it does not open, you get error messages) or viewing/downloading an attached file, please contact Yandex.Mail Support through the feedback from and attach the message identifier and screenshots to your request.

To find the message identifier, copy the identifier from the browser's address bar when reading messages.

← ⌕ https://mail.yandex.com/neo2/2450000008106692548

Notifications are not received from the site

If you do not receive a confirmation message after completing registration, please check the following:

- your email address at the site is correct;
- a rule for deleting messages is not configured in <u>mail processing rules</u>;
- the mail address of the site is missing in the blacklist.

If you are confident that mailbox settings are correct and that the address specified on the site is correct, then try to request a letter from the site again. If the message does not arrive within a few hours, please contact site administration.

Messages are delivered for other people.

Possible reasons for receiving messages for other people in your mailbox that include your or someone else's address in the **To** field:

- the sender made a mistake when specifying the recipient's address;
- fake recipient address in the email properties.

We (Yandex team) recommend that you simply ignore such letters.

Multiple Files Cannot be Attached Simultaneously.

If you are using Internet Explorer and cannot select multiple files for attachment when creating your message, make sure you have an up-to-date version of Adobe Flash Player installed. Open the page for downloading the module. If the version on your computer differs from the latest one, you will see the button **Install now** in the right part of the page. Click it to update the module.

You may have problems attaching files when using a proxy server to access the Internet.

Your authorization fails (you cannot log in with your username).

If you encounter a problem when you try to log in (enter your username and password), please carefully read the error message that also describes the methods for solutions.

If you see "Invalid username-password pair! Authorization failed", make sure you correctly entered login info, the Caps Lock key is not pressed, and the Latin keyboard layout is used. If you still cannot resolve the problem, please follow the password recovery instructions.

Incorrectly configured cookies in your browser may be another reason authorization failed. Read about cookies settings for your browser http://help.yandex.com/common/browsers-cookies.xml.

Username Restoration.

If you forgot your username, try to use the tip on the password recovery page. This tip may work if you recently logged into Yandex from the same computer.

Also try to get in touch with one of your addressees and ask him/her to send your email address or profile in one of the Yandex services (for example, "Moy Krug").

If you still cannot restore your username, contact Yandex.Mail Support through the feedback form.

Password Recovery.

If you forget your password, you can recover it on the password recovery page. Enter your username or email address, character from the picture and click **Next**. Depending on the details that you provided during registration and on the Personal information page, you will be automatically offered three password recovery options: an SMS code to a confirmed phone number, an answer to the security question, or an additional address.

Mail Security.

HTTPS Support

If you are using an insecure HTTP connection and unreliable communication channels (for example, public access points) for Internet access, information from your mailbox (personal correspondence, passwords, phone, and credit card numbers, etc.) may be intercepted by intruders.

Yandex.Mail uses HTTPS protocol to protect your mailbox. It provides security and confidentiality by encrypting your personal data before sending it to the server. HTTPS protocol is supported by all modern browsers.

Attention! If possible, avoid connecting your devices to public Internet access points that do not utilize HTTPS protocol.

To reduce the risk of data loss, use only reliable communication channels for Internet access which provide a secure HTTPS connection. If, for some reason, your Internet provider does not support this protocol, switch to a more reliable ISP.

If, while working in a network, you find that the safe HTTPS-connection is disabled, contact your system administrator to find out the causes for this and eliminate them.

Attention! If the HTTPS protocol is not working correctly, the problem may also be caused by viruses on your computer. If all settings are correct and the protocol is not blocked by your provider or administrator, check your computer with an antivirus.

Digital Signature.

DKIM (Domain Keys Identified Mail) is an email sender verification technology which adds a digital signature associated with a domain name. This signature confirms that the message has not been intercepted and modified after being sent from the sender's mail server.

The digital signature is designed to prove email authenticity and protects against spam and phishing. Messages are provided with a digital signature on the mail server of the email sender. The sender cannot add the signature themselves, unless they are the administrator of the server from which the email is being sent.

If you are reading messages and see a grey mark in the **From** field stating **Digital signature invalid**, you should treat the contents of the message cautiously.

To correctly display the digital signature, DKIM technology support is required from both parties (not just from the email recipient, but also the email sender). For this reason, invalid signatures from "honest" senders may raise a false alarm.

If you are completely confident about the sender and still see the invalid digital signature message, just ignore this alert. You can also contact Support at the sender's mail service to prevent the alert from causing false alarms in the future.

Mobile Phone Confirmation.

A confirmed mobile phone number is required to recover your password or receive notifications. If you forget your password, you can specify your phone number to receive a recovery code in SMS.

Note. If you do not use a mobile phone or Yandex does not support sending SMS to your operator, you can recover your forgotten password at <u>an additional email address</u> or by answering a security question.

Adding phone numbers

You can add your phone number on the <u>Phone numbers</u> page. Enter the number and click **Add** To confirm your number, enter the code sent in the SMS to your number and your Yandex password, and then click **Confirm**.

Note. SMS delivery time depends on your network operator and usually takes several minutes (maximum delivery time is 24 hours). If you do not receive the message, try requesting it again some time later.

Possible problems and troubleshooting tips

"Invalid number format"

The phone number should be entered using the following format: +7 YYY XXXXXXX, where +7 is the code for Russia, YYY is the code of your operator, XXXXXXX is the seven-digit number. For example: +7 123 456 78 90.

"This number is blocked."

Phone numbers are temporarily blocked after confirmation is sent. Wait for the SMS with the code and complete the confirmation procedure. If you do not receive the message, try requesting it again some time later.

The message with the confirmation code does not arrive.

Possible reasons:

- the system has not had enough time to process the sms-message (the maximum time for message delivery is 24 hours);
- your phone is switched off or beyond network coverage;
- you entered an incorrect telephone number;
- your operator is not supported by the Yandex message delivery system.

There are incoming messages about adding, changing or deleting the phone number

If you are trying to do something with the main phone number, just continue: For security reasons, Yandex sends electronic messages and SMS notifications about all operations.

If notification arrives unexpectedly, it means that someone has got access to your account. Do not be afraid: access can be easily restored automatically by means of the main phone number. Without access to your telephone, the intruder will only be able to delete or change the connected number after 30 days. During this time you will be able to do the following:

1. Restore access to the account and change the password.

Follow the link **Forgot your password?** and then follow the instructions in Yandex.Passport: get the recovery code and set a new password (when thinking about the password, consider <u>our guidelines</u>).

2. If you delete or change the main telephone number, the operation can be undone on the page <u>Phone numbers</u>.

Attention! If your phone number is already connected to three Yandex accounts and you link it to a fourth one, this number will be automatically unconnected from the three other accounts. Messages about these operations will arrive at the email addresses of these accounts.

Session History.

Yandex.Mail log stores the history of changes made in your mailbox, as well as IP addresses from which authorization was made.

Actions that have no visual implications (e.g., reading previously read mail, visiting a folder, etc.) are not displayed in the log.

You may view the data for the last 7 days (about 2,000 actions).

Attention! Session history contains reference information and makes it impossible to cancel executed actions (for example, to recover deleted emails).

To open the session history, click the **Last username** link at the bottom of the page (if the last change to the mailbox was made more than 15 minutes ago) or **Session history** (if less than 15 minutes have elapsed since the last modification).

You can also view the log from the menu **Settings** → **Security**.

The log shows your current IP address and other IP addresses under which you recently logged into this mailbox. All of the log's historical data is grouped by dates.

To view detailed information for any day from the list, click the link with the date. The list displays the time of the action, the IP address of the device from which the change was made, and the name of the action.

Your current IP-address — 2a02:6b8:0:2807:10fd:68a0:e805:7310

9 jun 2015	Login to Mail	18:29
	Login to Mail	18:16
	"From Spock" label removed	18:02 one message
	New message received	16:59 from comm.spock@yandex.com
	Login to Mail	16:57
	Login to Mail	16:44
	Login to Mail	16:33
8 jun 2015	Login to Mail	16:51
5 jun 2015	Login to Mail	18:29
	Login to Mail	18:13
	Login to Mail	18:03

Fraud Alert.

Yandex.Mail regularly detects dangerous and scam websites and scam mail, and marks suspicious messages with a special alert.

⚠ Yandex.Mail believes this message to be part of a phishing scam. (What does this mean?)
Do not reply to this message or follow any of the links.
We strongly recommend deleting this message immediately.

Delete this message

End of Topic.

A fresh topic

Keyboard Shortcuts in Yandex Mail.

Use the following list of keyboard shortcuts to enhance your productivity in Yandex.

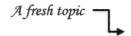

Action	Shortcut
Show the list of keyboard shortcuts	?
Check for mail	F9
Print	Ctrl + P
Find a message	/

Lists of Folders, Messages, and Labels.

Action	Shortcut
Go to "Inbox"	Ctrl + I
Switch between folders and labels	↑ and ↓
Collapse or expand a list of subfolders (for the selected folder)	Space
Move to the adjacent column	← and →
Previous message (in the list of messages)	↑
Next message (in the list of messages)	↓
Expand or collapse a conversation (for the selected message in the list of messages)	Enter
Open the selected message	Enter
Select or deselect several messages at once	Shift + ↑ and Shift + ↓
Select all messages	Ctrl + A
Label the selected messages	L
Move the selected messages to a folder	M
Mark the selected messages as read	Q
Mark the selected messages as unread	U
Forward the selected messages	F
Mark the selected messages as important	I
Delete the selected messages	Delete
Show the important messages	I
Show the unread messages	U
Previous page	Ctrl + ←
Next page	Ctrl + →

Creating a New Message.

Action	Shortcut
Write a message	W, C
Attach a file	+
Send a message	Ctrl + Enter
Save a message as a draft	Ctrl + S

Read a Message.

Action	Shortcut
Mark a message as unread	Shift + U
Mark or unmark a message as "spam"	Shift + S
Mark or unmark a message as "important"	Shift + I
Label a message	Shift + L
Move a message to a folder	Shift + M
Forward a message	Shift + F
Reply	Shift + E
Reply to all	Shift + R
Remove	Delete
Archive all attachments	Ctrl + S
Previous message	P or N
Next message	J or K

Personalized Buttons.

Action	Shortcut
Archive	A
Forward	Alt + F
Move to folder	Alt + M
Label	Alt + L

| Autoreply | Alt + R |

General.

Action	Shortcut
Show the list of keyboard shortcuts	?
Check for mail	Shift + O
Print	Shift + P
Find a message	/

Lists of Folders, Messages, and Labels.

Action	Shortcut
Switch between folders or labels	↑ and ↓
Collapse or expand a list of subfolders (for the selected folder)	Space
Move to the adjacent column	← and →
Go to "Inbox"	Cmd + I
Previous message (in the list of messages)	↑
Next message (in the list of messages)	↓
Expand or collapse a conversation (for the selected message in the list of messages)	Enter
Open the selected message	Enter
Select or deselect several messages at once	Shift + ↑ and Shift + ↓
Select all messages	Cmd + A
Label the selected messages	L
Move the selected messages to a folder	M

Mark the selected messages as read	Q
Mark the selected messages as unread	U
Forward the selected messages	F
Mark the selected messages as important	I
Delete the selected messages	Cmd + Backspace
Show the important messages	I
Show the unread messages	U
Previous page	Ctrl + ←
Next page	Ctrl + →

Creating a New Message.

Action	Shortcut
Write a message	W, C
Attach a file	+
Send a message	Cmd + Enter
Save a message as a draft	Cmd + S

Read a Message.

Action	Shortcut
Mark a message as unread	Shift + U
Mark or unmark a message as "spam"	Shift + S
Mark or unmark a message as "important"	Shift + I
Label a message	Shift + L
Move a message to a folder	Shift + M
Forward a message	Shift + F

Reply	Shift + E
Reply to all	Shift + R
Remove	Cmd + Backspace
Archive all attachments	Cmd + S
Previous message	P or N
Next message	J or K

Personalized Buttons.

Action	Shortcut
Archive	A
Forward	Alt + F
Move to folder	Alt + M
Label	Alt + L
Autoreply	Alt + R

To quickly access a list of all keyboard shortcuts, use the **?** key.

To disable keyboard shortcuts:

1. Go to **Settings** ⚙ → **Miscellaneous**.
2. Disable the **Use keyboard shortcuts** option.
3. Save the changes.

CHAPTER 11.

Tips, Tricks, Techniques, and Keyboard Shortcuts for use in Zoho mail.

Introduction: This is a free and paid email service provided by Zoho Corporation.

A fresh topic

Features of Zoho Email.

Ad-Free, Clean, Fast Interface.

There are no ads displayed in Zoho Mail's web mail interface, ever. Not even in free plans. This means total respect for user privacy as your messages are not scanned for keywords to feed you ads. However, freedom from annoying ads is not the stand out feature in Zoho Mail. It's the wide range of options to organize and categorize your messages. This includes familiar items like folders and labels, flags, automatic filters, as well as one-of-a-kind capabilities, like the thread nesting style conversation view.

- Familiar Interface

- Multi-level Folders
- Drag and Drop
- Rules and Filters
- Mass Selection
- Filtered Views
- Threaded View
- Tabbed Views

Feature Packed for Business & Professional Use.

Zoho Mail's webmail interface has been designed to break the notion that only desktop email clients can provide the power features favored by business users. Your users will find the familiar functionality of desktop email blended perfectly with the convenience and flexibility of browser-based access. This means you get the best of both worlds.

- Manage multiple accounts
- Dynamic 'From' addresses
- Customized account personalities
- Advanced Search
- Anti Spam and Anti Virus
- Instant Chat
- Templates
- Shortcuts

- Outbox

Go Beyond Email. Take Your Office Online

Gone are the days of software installations and upgrades. Take your office to the cloud. Zoho Mail comes bundled with Zoho Docs, a comprehensive online office and document management suite that runs from within a web browser. Your users can create, edit and collaborate on word documents, spreadsheets and presentations; online. Along with integrated calendar, tasks, notes and contacts modules, Zoho Mail provides the best tools to improve productivity and efficiency.

- Docs
- Calendar
- Tasks
- Notes
- Contacts

Anywhere, Anytime Access

The biggest advantage of email hosted on the cloud is that you get to access your messages on the move. Be it through your mobile, laptop or desktop, as long as there is an internet connection - present almost anywhere, anytime these days - keep your email exchanges and communications flowing.

- Web access
- Desktop access
- Mobile access

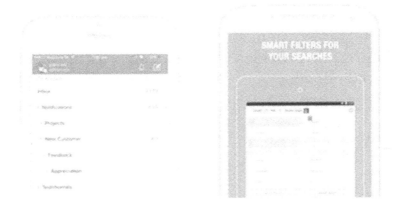

Extensive Control Panel.

Your IT administrators will find it a breeze to set up and manage emailing for your business with the extensive control panel interface. Representing the entire back end of your email hosting account, administrators can easily control individual user mailbox quota and privileges, email policies, group email accounts and other such aspects from within this centralized control center.

- Domain management
- User account & access management
- Email policy management
- Group management
- SAML authentication
- Allowed IPs

Free, Expert Aided Migration Options.

The task of migrating from your existing email solution is simple without laborious setup, loss of time, or loss of productivity. A self-service migration module is a few clicks away in the control panel. Lightweight software tools are available for Exchange server and Outlook PST migrations. Zoho's support experts will coordinate with you throughout the process to ensure your switch is smooth. And to top it all up, they do not charge extra for migration assistance.

- IMAP/POP migration
- Exchange Server
- Outlook PST

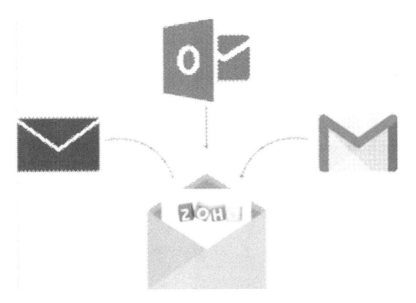

Email & CRM Integration.

Businesses of all sizes are doing the smart thing of setting up a CRM application for their sales and marketing teams, enabling them to work more efficiently. At the same time, habits die hard and people still rely on good old email for communicating with clients, prospects and customers. What do you do? If you made the wise decision of choosing Zoho CRM for your business, you'll be amazed with the contextual gadgets feature in Zoho Mail. It's like having CRM inside your email.

End of Topic.

A fresh topic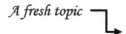

Keyboard Shortcuts in Zoho Email.

If you are a key-savvy user, you can now use keyboard shortcuts for the most repeated actions you perform in Zoho Mail. Moreover, you can even customize the keyboard shortcuts to match your requirements. For example you may configure the combination 'in' to go to the Inbox instead of 'gi' , 'se' to go to the sent items instead of gs, 'lab' to view the labeled items (first label in your list) etc instead of the standard Keyboard Shortcuts used earlier. Using Keyboard shortcuts makes your mailing tasks easier, reducing the number of clicks.

If you are just comfortable using mouse and do not need keyboard shortcuts, you have an option to disable Keyboard shortcuts.

1. Click Settings.
2. Go To Mail Settings » Keyboard Shortcuts
3. Select Enable to Enable the Keyboard Shortcuts

4. To change any of the default shortcut keys configured, click on the Text box
5. Provide the preferred Key combination for the corresponding action
   - A maximum of 3 characters will be accepted
   - You cannot repeat the same key sets for different actions
6. Click Save to Save the settings

Note:

- You cannot repeat the same key sets for different actions

1. The default shortcuts work irrespective of the Enabled or Disabled state of the Keyboard Shortcuts.
2. The table below shows the default actions and the default shortcuts which cannot be disabled.

Use the following list of keyboard shortcuts to enhance your productivity in Zoho mail.

Default Keyboard Shortcuts (Cannot be Disabled).

Shortcut	Action
Up arrow (?)	Read Previous Message
Down arrow (?)	Read Next Message
Left arrow (?)	Expand Folder
Right arrow (?)	Collapse Folder
Esc	Clear menu

The Keyboard shortcuts in the following table can be disabled, however are predefined and cannot be customized. If you disable keyboard shortcuts, the shortcuts listed in the below tables will be disabled and will not work.

Predefined Keyboard Shortcuts.

Shortcut	Action
Ctrl + enter	Send message
Ctrl + Shift + enter	Send message immediately
Ctrl + s	Save draft
Ctrl + Shift + y	Save Template

The Keyboard shortcuts available before customization are listed below. You can click and edit the key combination in the Keyboard Shortcuts page, for the actions to customize as per your preference.

Customizable Keyboard Shortcuts.

Shortcut	Action
C	Compose
/	Search
R	Reply
A	Reply All
F	Forward
.	Open Mark as menu
S	Show the original message content
T	Open message in new tab
O	Open message in new window
\	Close preview
M	Fetch new messages (Refresh)

D	Move to
!	Report as spam
?	Open shortcut menu
Esc	Clear menu
Y	Clear label
Shift + p	Print message
Shift + u	Mark as unread
Shift + i	Mark as read
Del	Delete message
L	Labels
E	Edit as new
Shift + a	Archive
Go to	
g then *i*	Go to Inbox
g then *u*	Go to Unread view
g then *s*	Go to Sent messages
g then *d*	Go to Draft
g then *f*	Go to Flagged messages
g then *a*	Go to All messages
g then l	Go to labeled messages
Selection	
X	Select message
Ctrl + a	Select all messages
Ctrl + d	Deselect all messages
Navigation	
P	Read previous message
N	Read next message
G	Expand folder
K	Collapse folder
Ctrl + [	Navigate through tabs-right to left
Ctrl +]	Navigate through tabs-left to right
*Ctrl + *	Close tab

CHAPTER 12.

Tips, Tricks, Techniques, and Keyboard Shortcuts for use in Hushmail.

Introduction: Hushmail is a web-based email service offering PGP-encrypted e-mail and vanity domain service. Hushmail offers "free" and "paid" versions of service. Hushmail uses OpenPGP standards and the source is available for download.
-Wikipedia.

A fresh topic

Features of Hushmail.

Email and Encryption in one Solution.

With Hushmail, you are able to send and receive emails as with any regular email service, but you also have the option to encrypt your emails for extra protection. The encryption is automatic between Hushmail users. For everyone else, you can manage it with a checkbox located on the Compose screen of webmail or Hushmail for iPhone app.

Hushmail can be used immediately without installing any software or hardware because it is a fully hosted web-based service. Access your email from anywhere via a web browser or by setting up your account on Hushmail for iPhone or on your favorite smartphone or PC email app.

Easy Encryption.

Encryption between Hushmail users happens automatically, so you don't even have to think about it. When emailing people who don't use Hushmail, our on-demand encryption is easily managed with a checkbox. Just sign in to your account on webmail or Hushmail for iPhone app, compose a message and check the "Encrypted" box to send the message securely. Learn how it works.

Multiple layers of security.

Hushmail has a proven track record of providing industry-standard OpenPGP encryption to protect the contents of the email, ensuring its security, privacy, and authenticity. In addition, all communications between you and hushmail servers use a secure connection (their A+ grade SSL/TLS connection is rated by Qualsys SSL Labs).

Two-step verification.

This layer of security prevents unauthorized access to your Hushmail account by using a two-stage process to authenticate your identity from any device they don't recognize. The first step is to sign in using your username and passphrase. The second step is entering a verification code that they'll send to your mobile phone or an alternate email address. You can also obtain a verification code using a smartphone app.

Send encrypted email to anyone.

Email sensitive information directly to your intended recipients, regardless of their email provider. They will be able to reply directly to your message and send documents securely, even if they don't have a Hushmail account.

Encrypted email on your iPhone.

Hushmail for iPhone lets you take the secure email experience of Hushmail with you anywhere you go. The app supports encrypted email to anyone, two-step verification, Touch ID, multiple accounts and aliases, and it's synced with your webmail account, for seamless access to contacts and settings.

Accessible everywhere you work.

Access your Hushmail account from the web or Hushmail for iPhone app. You can also set up your Hushmail account on your favorite smartphone email app or email software of your choice on your PC (e.g. Outlook, Apple Mail, or Thunderbird) with Hushmail's POP/IMAP support.

Use your own domain

Personalize your email using the domain that you already own (e.g. yourbusiness.com) and remain as professional and trustworthy as ever. If you don't own a domain, you can use one of our ".hush.com" subdomains (e.g. yourname@yourbusiness.hush.com). This feature is only available in Hushmail business plans.

Dedicated customer support

If you need help with Hushmail, you can always call, email, or chat with them. They will take the time to personally answer all your questions, understand your problem and do their best to find a solution.

Unlimited email aliases

Aliases are alternate email addresses ending in @nym.hush.com. Use these aliases to mask your real email address when you don't feel comfortable disclosing it. Aliases point email to your existing Hushmail account and share the same inbox.

Business model built around privacy

Privacy is the priority of Husmail team, not an afterthought. When you use Hushmail, you own your data and your emails are not analyzed to display advertising. Your data is never sold to anyone. Your IP address does not appear on the headers of the email.

Data safely stored in Canada

Location matters. The rules that apply to the protection of your data differ from one location to another. Enjoy some peace of mind, safe in the knowledge that your data is stored only in Canada and under the protection of Canadian Law.

Secure forms

Securely receive confidential information collected on your website. This feature is available in Hushmail Healthcare and Legal plans.

Manage users

Set up, delete, and configure user accounts with Hush Tools, their administration panel. This feature is available in their business plans.

Email archiving

Keeps a record of all emails sent and received by all users in your domain. This feature is available in their business plans.

Catch-all email addresses

Choose one of your accounts to receive all email sent to addresses in your domain that do not exist. This feature is available in their business plans.

Email forwarding

Create email addresses like info@example.com that are automatically redirected to name@example.com. This feature is available in their business plans.

How do you want to use Hushmail?

For Business

Protect your trade secrets and customer data with a solution that accommodates all your email needs.

For Personal Use

Keep your personal conversations private and enjoy an inbox with no ads.

End of Topic.

A fresh topic ⌐

Most Commonly Used Keyboard Shortcuts in Hushmail

Use the following list of keyboard shortcuts to enhance your productivity in Hushmail.

Shortcuts for Open New Message:

Action	Shortcut
Open a message	Ctrl+O
Create new message (when in Mail)	Ctrl+N
Create new message	Ctrl+Shift+M

Navigation Shortcut Keys:

Action	Shortcut
Switch to inbox	Ctrl+Shift+I

Switch to outbox	Ctrl+Shift+O
Open address book	Ctrl+Shift+B
Open a folder list	Ctrl+Y
Read next message (with a message open)	Ctrl+. (period)
Read previous message (with a message open)	Ctrl+, (comma)
Read previous message (with a message open)	F6

Shortcut Keys for Changing Messages:

Action	Shortcut
Delete open item	Ctrl+D
Mark as read	Ctrl+Q
Mark as unread	Ctrl+U
Find or replace (with a message open)	F4
Find next (with a message open)	Shift+F4
Print	Ctrl+P
Mark for download	Ctrl+Alt+M
Clear Mark for Download	Ctrl+Alt+U
Mark as not junk mail	Ctrl+Alt+J
Toggle follow-up flag	Insert

Tools:

Action	Shortcut
Check for new mail	F9

Display send/receive progress	Ctrl+B
Send mail	Alt+S
Reply to selected message	Ctrl+R
Reply all	Ctrl+Shift+R
Forward selected mail	Ctrl+F
Forward as attachment	Ctrl+Alt+F

CHAPTER 13.

Tips, Tricks, Techniques, and Keyboard Shortcuts for use in Gmail.

Introduction: This is a free email service created by Paul Buchheit, owned and sold by Google, and launched in 2004.

A fresh topic

Tips & Tricks in Gmail.

Check out the tips below to help you get started with Gmail.

Check out the categories in your inbox

Your emails are automatically organized into tabs. For example, an email about a sale from a shopping site can be found in the "Promotions" tab.

Choose a theme for your inbox

You can choose an image for your inbox background. To get started, click Settings ⚙ > **Themes**.

Find your emails

Use the Search box to quickly find your emails. Inside the search box, click the Down arrow to filter your results ▼ .

Organize your emails with labels

Labels are like folders, but you can add more than one label to a message. To add a label to an email, select the email, then click Labels ◗. The label will be shown next to the email.

Open & download attachments

You'll see a preview of attachments sent to you at the bottom of your email. Click the preview to see the attachment, download it, print it, and more.

Undo sending a message

Turn on Undo Send to get extra time to look at an email before it gets delivered.

Automatically manage incoming emails

Filters can do things like automatically label, archive, delete, star, and forward your incoming emails.

Start a video call

When you add someone to your Hangouts chat list, you can start a video call with them from your inbox by hovering over their name and clicking Video call ■ .

Check emails from all your accounts

If you use multiple accounts, you can check all your emails in Gmail. You can also send messages from an address that isn't your Gmail address.

End of Topic.

A fresh topic

Keyboard Shortcuts for Gmail.

Save time navigating in Gmail by using keyboard shortcuts.

Turn on Keyboard Shortcuts

Some keyboard shortcuts only work if you've turned them on.

Note: Keyboard shortcuts aren't supported on all keyboards.

1. Open <u>Gmail</u>.
2. In the top right, click Settings ⚙.
3. Click **Settings**.
4. Scroll down to the "Keyboard shortcuts" section.
5. Select **Keyboard shortcuts on**.
6. At the bottom of the page, click **Save Changes**.

Shortcuts you can use

You can use keyboard shortcuts to navigate your inbox and messages, format text, and complete actions like archiving and deleting.

To see a complete list of keyboard shortcuts, including which need to be turned on, type **?** When you have Gmail open.

Note: Keyboard shortcuts work differently on PC and Mac computers. On PCs, you'll use **Ctrl** instead of ⌘.

Use the following list of keyboard shortcuts to enhance your productivity in Google mail.

Compose & Chat.

Action	Shortcut
Previous message in an open conversation	P
Next message in an open conversation	N
Focus main window	Shift + Esc
Focus latest chat or compose	Esc
Advance to the next chat or compose	Ctrl + .
Advance to previous chat or compose	Ctrl + ,
Send	⌘/Ctrl + Enter
Add cc recipients	⌘/Ctrl + Shift + c
Add bcc recipients	⌘/Ctrl + Shift + b
Access custom from	⌘/Ctrl + Shift + f
Insert a link	⌘/Ctrl + k

Go to previous misspelled word	⌘/Ctrl + ;
Go to next misspelled word	⌘/Ctrl + '
Open spelling suggestions	⌘/Ctrl + m

Formatting Text.

Action	Shortcut
Previous font	⌘/Ctrl + Shift + 5
Next font	⌘/Ctrl + Shift + 6
Decrease text size	⌘/Ctrl + Shift + -
Increase text size	⌘/Ctrl + Shift and +
Bold	⌘/Ctrl + b
Italics	⌘/Ctrl + i
Underline	⌘/Ctrl + u
Numbered list	⌘/Ctrl + Shift + 7
Bulleted list	⌘/Ctrl + Shift + 8
Quote	⌘/Ctrl + Shift + 9
Indent less	⌘/Ctrl + [
Indent more	⌘/Ctrl +]
Align left	⌘/Ctrl + Shift + l
Align center	⌘/Ctrl + Shift + e
Align right	⌘/Ctrl + Shift + r
Set right-to-left	⌘/Ctrl + Shift + ,
Set left-to-right	⌘/Ctrl + Shift + .
Remove formatting	⌘/Ctrl + \

Actions.

Note: These shortcuts won't work unless keyboard shortcuts are turned on.

Action	Shortcut
Move focus to toolbar	,
Select conversation	x
Toggle star/rotate among superstars	s
Remove label	y
Archive	e
Mute conversation	m
Report as spam	!
Delete	#
Reply	r
Open in a new window	Shift + r
Reply all	a
Reply all in a new window	Shift + a
Forward	f
Forward in a new window	Shift + f
Update conversation	Shift + n
Remove conversation from current view and go previous/next	] or [
Archive conversation and go to previous/next	} or {
Undo last action	z
Mark as read	Shift + i
Mark as unread	Shift + u
Mark unread from the selected message	_
Mark as important	+ or =
Mark as not important	-
Expand entire conversation	;
Collapse entire conversation	:
Add conversation to Tasks	Shift + t

Hangouts.

Note: These keyboard shortcuts won't work unless keyboard shortcuts are turned on.

Action	Shortcut
Show menu	h + m
Show archived hangouts	h + a
Show Hangout requests	h + i
Focus on the conversation list	h + c
Open phone	g + p **or** h + p

Jumping.

Note: These keyboard shortcuts won't work unless keyboard shortcuts are turned on.

Action	Shortcut
Go to Inbox	g + i
Go to Starred conversations	g + s
Go to Sent messages	g + t
Go to Drafts	g + d
Go to All mail	g + a
Go to Contacts	g + c
Go to Tasks	g + k
Go to label	g + l

Threadlist Selection.

Note: These keyboard shortcuts won't work unless keyboard shortcuts are turned on.

Action	Shortcut
Select all conversations	* + a
Deselect all conversations	* + n
Select read conversations	* + r
Select unread conversations	* + u
Select starred conversations	* + s
Select unstarred conversations	* + t

Navigation.

Note: These keyboard shortcuts won't work unless keyboard shortcuts are turned on.

Action	Shortcut
Back to threadlist	U
New conversation	K
Older conversation	J
Open conversation	o **or** Enter
Go to next Inbox section	`
Go to previous Inbox section	~

Application.

Note: These keyboard shortcuts won't work unless keyboard shortcuts are turned on.

Action	Shortcut
Compose	C
Compose in a new tab	D
Search mail	/
Search chat contacts	G
Open "more actions" menu	.
Open "move to" menu	V
Open "label as" menu	L
Open keyboard shortcut help	?

Customer's Page.

This page is for customers who enjoyed Top 10 Email Service Providers Keyboard Shortcuts.

Dear beautiful customer, we will feel honoured to have you review this book if you enjoyed or found it useful. We also advise you to get the ebook version of this book in order to access the numerous useful links included in it. Thanks for your co-operation.

Download Our EBooks Today For Free.

In order to appreciate our customers, we have made some of our titles available at 0.00. They are totally free. Feel free to get a copy of the free titles.

Here are books we give to our customers free of charge:

(A) For Keyboard Shortcuts in Windows check:

Windows 7 Keyboard Shortcuts.

(B) For Keyboard Shortcuts in Office 2016 for Windows check:

Word 2016 Keyboard Shortcuts For Windows.

(C) For Keyboard Shortcuts in Office 2016 for Mac check:

OneNote 2016 Keyboard Shortcuts For Macintosh.

Follow <u>this link</u> to download any of the titles listed above for free.

Note: Feel free to download them from our website or your favorite bookstore today. Thank you.

Other Books By This Publisher.

Titles for single programs under Shortcut Matters Series are not included in this list.

S/N	Title	Series
Series A: Limits Breaking Quotes.		
1	Discover Your Key Christian Quotes	Limits Breaking Quotes
Series B: Shortcut Matters.		
1	Windows 7 Shortcuts	Shortcut Matters
2	Windows 7 Shortcuts & Tips	Shortcut Matters
3	Windows 8.1 Shortcuts	Shortcut Matters
4	Windows 10 Shortcut Keys	Shortcut Matters
5	Microsoft Office 2007 Keyboard Shortcuts For Windows.	Shortcut Matters
6	Microsoft Office 2010 Shortcuts For Windows.	Shortcut Matters
7	Microsoft Office 2013 Shortcuts For Windows.	Shortcut Matters
8	Microsoft Office 2016 Shortcuts For Windows.	Shortcut Matters
9	Microsoft Office 2016 Keyboard Shortcuts For Macintosh.	Shortcut Matters
10	Top 11 Adobe Programs Keyboard Shortcuts	Shortcut Matters
11	Hot Corel Programs Keyboard Shortcuts	Shortcut Matters
12	Top 10 Browsers Keyboard Shortcuts	Shortcut Matters
Series C: Teach Yourself.		

1	Teach Yourself Computer Fundamentals	Teach Yourself
2	Teach Yourself Computer Fundamentals Workbook	Teach Yourself

Series D: For Painless Publishing

1	Self-Publish it with CreateSpace.	For Painless Publishing
2	Where is my money? Now solved for Kindle and CreateSpace	For Painless Publishing
3	Describe it on Amazon	For Painless Publishing
4	How To Market That Book.	For Painless Publishing

www.ingramcontent.com/pod-product-compliance
Lightning Source LLC
LaVergne TN
LVHW022302060326
832902LV00020B/3229